Journeys with the Alchemists & Alternative Spiritual Masters.

Original Translations, Observations, and Applications, by Russell Yoder

Copyright Russell R. Yoder 2018
All Rights Reserved
First Paperback Edition

The Hex Factory
2080 East Cumberland Street
Philadelphia, PA
19125
www.thehexfactory.com

ISBN-13:
978-1729593851

ISBN-10:
1729593852

Table of Contents

Forward..9

From German Pietism to a Universal Heritage:
Some Brief Remarks..11

HOW TO ATTAIN THE SOLAR BODY: THE SECRET
TRANSMISSION OF JACOB BOEHME..17

How to Practice "Magia" (the Contemplative
Philosopher's Stone}..22

Alchemical Diary Entry of the Swedish
Behmenist, Erik Eriksson ....'...27

GOLD FROM MIDNIGHT: A Thorough
Description of the Supreme Jewel of the World 33

The Potable Gold of the Ancients..65

Master Alchemist Khunrath: As Practiced from
a Vajrayana Perspective..77

A Brief Investigation of an Initiatory Model:
Swedenborg's 'Asian Society 82

THE SPRING EQUINOX SELF-ENACTED ELUS COHEN RITE OF
RECONCILIATION & ADOPTION..89

PERSONAL INSTRUCTION WORK IN THE PRESENCE OF
THE SOVEREIGN ALONE: FOR ANY DAY OF THE WEEK
WHATSOEVER. (TRANSLATED FROM THE "MANUSCRIT D'ALGER")........96

""HEDGE WIZARD": SELECTED VERSES OF
RUSSELL YODER...100

AXIS MUNDI WITHIN THE OUROBOROS OCEAN"
(A CREATIVE ADAPTATION OF PGM IV)...106

Buried in the Breast (a Tale of Northwest Passage)
Alternative Realilty Fiction..108

About the Author...121

A note from the Editor...122

FOREWORD by the Author/Translator

My roots are in the radical Pietist tradition of Ephrata and the Universalist tradition of my Family's ancestral mentor and mage, George de Benneville. Common to both aspects of this heritage is an awareness of "alchemy" as a tool for effecting physical and spiritual change in our perceived reality -- perception being the key, of course; or as our seminal source of inspiration, Jacob Boehme has it,"our world must be made heaven, and heaven the world." Such an effectual outlook requires a wholistic approach, but its ground or foundation can be laid nowhere other than, or prior to, what is raised up as a newborn clarity in ourselves. The alchemists were savvy and self-honest enough to know that, first, our dark nights of faulty mis or pre-conception had to be dissolved and dispensed with; in order to conceive a Pearl of genuine worth. For even abiding within seemingly "right traditions" can be exposed as an iron-cold sarcophagus, leading to "death" rather than gold; as the alternate-reality "dream" of my experience at a latter day outpost of Ephrata suggests.* But if we die to those constricting parameters, whatever their nature, breakthrough does occur and precise insights emerge; because our alchemically-forged faculties have themselves become the light!** What you will find herein, then, are pithy penetrations of such light; offered by me as practical handles for engaging the wonderful realizations of those predecessor spiritual masters and practitioners, who, like us, aspired to a self-clarifying and world reconciling awareness.

Russell R. Yoder

Thailand, 2018

---

* Recorded in the form of a short story as the last piece here, the title is a quotation from the Rosicrucian manifesto, Fama Fraternitatis.

** "For then all sense organs, and their respective sense objects, are Light only.(Guhyasamaja-tantra)

From German Pietism to a Universal Heritage: Some Brief Remarks

"Ideologically speaking, we find in the members of the Gold- und Rosenkreutz, pietistic and vitalistic conceptions of a correspondence between gold, the sun and God, and a belief in a vital spirit conveyed by the blood which is the basis of a miraculous medicine and tincture for metals." (The Quest for the Phoenix: Spiritual Alchemy and Rosicrucianism, by Hereward Tilton, p. 252)

Let me very briefly here consider the relevance to a universal heritage, of the Solar-Christ-Philosophical Gold symbolism found in old German pietist and alchemical literature. I think it is especially important to highlight some essentials of this, because the tradition has long since been jettisoned from mainstream Christianity; and can perhaps at last be spoken of as a bridge to more inclusive methods of realization.

Although the primary sources of the tradition are often regarded as especially recondite, buried within the weighty works of Jacob Boehme, the essential word-associations we wish to consider, are straightforward enough: 1.) the image from Genesis, of the Waters that are "Above the Firmament" 2.) the equating of spiritual Sun-Christ-Potable Gold, and Oil or Blood 3.) and the equating of the Moon (or Luna) with the Sublunar spirit of the earth and air. Uniquely, what is received from "above" the firmament is a *fluid transfusion* of Life that in elementary terms is "drinkable"; as in the alchemical *aurum potabile,* literally "drinkable gold". We will see throughout our brief index of the pietist vocabulary, an ingestion, imbibition, and saturation of one Principle by another.

Indeed, Boehme highlights the ground for us, by saying that the Firmament (and the Water Above the Firmament) is "another Principle" from our ordinary conscious world, and "has another birth (that is, another life) than the external elementary life has." And yet, the readiest analogue of this "Other" may be found within the hard compaction of the stones and earth itself, where there is "an Oil" which is "sweeter than any sugar can be." Whoever can "unloose" this Oil from its hard moorings "has the Pearl of the whole World." (Clearly, we step into the realm of alchemy here, which is wholly *consistent* with the pietist approach, and *not* a mixed metaphor!)

But there is a catch also. Unless one is already *in* the "new birth" of the "Other" Principle, access to it is not possible; *except* for the rare instance of it being manually received from an already-accomplished Master (*see* Boehme's twenty-third epistle). Therefore, the *surest* route to it is to develop a genuine *thirst* for the "Other Principle". Then, Boehme says, it is possible to go into one's "Luna", the *dry* sublunar earth and air of our being, with the Oil "of Christ's heavenly Blood" (in the pietist rendering); which is also the potable Gold "of the Waters Above".

Our individual "Saturation" points may differ, but a useful formula is provided in the Threefold Life of Man: "Give your Luna a little of Sol, but if its hunger and thirst be great, give it a seventh part of Sol; then it is complete." The "angel brothers" in Amsterdam applied this formula to a schema of their subtle centers somewhat like the seven chakras. They discovered that ONE of these centers in particular thirsts for "a seventh part of Sol", in order to illuminate the others.

OPENING such a center in turn unleashes a "flood" of effectiveness! The famous theosophical correspondence of Kirchberger and Saint-Martin, refers to the "angel brother" Gichtel as a GENERAL, who defeated the military generals of Louis XIV when they attacked the city of Amsterdam from various quarters in 1672. The potency of the cross which radiated from Gichtel's center on this occasion was as great as the more peaceful projections envisioned by the alchemists. (Letter LVIII. Morat, 25th October 1794)

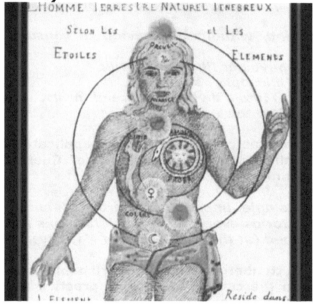

The centers of nature that the angel brothers sought to illuminate and transmute (from their manual, Practical Theosophy)

Needless to say then, the Spiritual infusion of our being is the Highest form of magic. Nagarjuna, the 2nd historical Buddha, plainly states that the transformation of both substances and circumstances is achieved solely by the force which flows from this core.

But the alchemist George von Welling says that the Gold at the core of our being (Hebrew, *Sahaph Aphar*), was *forfeited* and replaced by "dry earth" (Hebrew, *Erez*) at the time of Man's Fall. The *solution* to such a condition, for the pietist mindset, is obvious. And we find a striking instance of such practical application in the chapbook pietism of the "Rosicrucian duke", Ernst August of Saxe-Weimar. Every prayer and homily of his is literally *dripping* with the flavor of another "inflowing" Principle:

O Lord Jesu! You incomprehensible living and eternal Sun-bread!
You saturate our mind, without our having to consume You.
As earthly bread, we have our fill of Your Will;
but as the heavenly Philosopher's Stone,
You transform Yourself into a divine Sun-bread for us.
Only to the lowly are You this overflowing Sea

In an even more remarkable example of such application, Susanna von Klettenberg, the pietist mentor of Goethe, confided to another luminary of her Age (Lavater):

I have received a single imperishable drop of aurum potabile, which transforms everything, which fashions me, as my Head is fashioned (at the Right Hand of Majesty).

But Fraulein von Klettenberg's single imperishable drop may also be found in the central meditative practice and experience of *Shingon,* the Japanese version of Vajrayana Buddhism. Here, "a single golden A-syllable", the Sanskrit equivalent of "Alpha and Omega" (and *essence* of the Buddhist saviour, Amida) is seen to manifest inside a visualized *Moon,* emitting a white radiance that dissolves and reshapes our world *anew*. Perhaps, a slightly updated Western approximation of this *same* effect may be had, by imagining our own "parched" condition (in the manner of von Welling's "Erez"), *transfused* with veins of a living gold, flowing *rivulets* that literally "grow" a vital new form within the old one!

These examples are admittedly succinct, but hopefully enough has been said here to suggest the value of preserving both the "pietist" mindset and vocabulary, as a more *general* or universal resource for transformative practices today.

HOW TO ATTAIN THE SOLAR BODY: THE SECRET TRANSMISSION OF JACOB BOEHME, IN A NEW TRANSLATION BY RUSSELL YODER FROM THE ORIGINAL GERMAN OF EPISTLE 15 (DENOTED AS NO. 22 IN EARLIER ENGLISH EDITIONS)

As many are not even aware of it, I have decided to post my translation of what is clearly Boehme's confidential transmission to a known contact of his. I regard it as clear evidence of his initiatory mentoring of certain individuals, which at the same time also affords *us* a glimpse of those observable and predictable manifestations that are generated interiorly through images relating us back to the 'Ancient of Days': ultimately enabling a divinely-intended reconciliation and replication by way of our entire internal chemistry.

"Regarding our secret intercourse, as you are aware, you must still be patient for a considerable time in this faithful process, and no other in the beginning. To see this process to its end may well require seven years; because it must be opened or digested by all six Properties of the Spiritual ground. Even if it is already opened by the Sun, the Key is hardly come into the first or second degree of the Center of Nature. For every property among the six Forms of the Spirit-life has a special Sun within itself, from the force and origin of the Light of Nature, as the essential Sun; and is opened up in order, as its birth and origin, or primal state, is. Saturn's Sun, through the Key of the outward sun, is unlocked, so that one sees the existing divergences of Nature: by Jupiter's Sun, one sees the power as a blossoming Tree, and hither you are come. If Mars is opened as the fiery Soul, Virgin Venus appears in her white dress and jests or frolics with the Soul: She goes out and in, up and down, with the Soul, to see whether it can be moved to the desire of Love; and of its own will wants to reintroduce the volatile qualities whereby the Soul has gone out of temperance or temperature into the volatile life of the destructive qualities; in order that Virgin Venus may be ensouled again, and get the Fire of the Tincture, in which her joy and life are restored. Virgin Venus is understood as the white Reflection-glass of the Sun at this place: but the Power of shining is not her own; for her property is the spiritual Water which originates from the Fire; since the separation in the Salnitre is in Mars' Sun.

So Virgin Venus separates herself, and covers herself with a copper skirt; because Mars wants her property, but he sullies her too much in his malice, and throws earth, soot and rust upon her, because he cannot help it. For he must give her the property of his own Fire-will, and he does not want to; so they argue for a long time: they are Spouses, but mutually unfaithful to each other. So then comes the Sun, and Mercury's Sun will rise, which is the fourth Key; and you shall have great Wonders, how God created Heaven and Earth, which is the Foundation of all Four Elements. And if you will be careful, you will see your own Genius before you, and see how the Word became Man, as the spoken Word; and how Virgin Venus became in its re-pronouncing in the existing divergences of forces, embraced and taken within these and changed into their purple color: They want to murder, but she is their baptism to the new life in this place. The fifth Key is Virgin Venus herself since she opens up her God as the Sun, and gives her will and beautiful garland or chaplet to the murderers; so that she stands as a slave. The Artist now imagines he has the new Child, but is still far from Birth of the same! The sixth Key is the Moon, when the Sun is shining upon it; so Mars, Jupiter, Saturn each must leave their will, and let their fleeting splendor sink: then the Moon in the Sun takes them into the Incarnation; the Artist suspects that he has lost there, but his hope will not be confounded. The Moon in its opened-up Sun is hungry for the right Sun, which going by force into it startles it in the wrath, and subdues it in its own right: then Virgin Venus seizes it and sinks into it with her Love. Mars in Jupiter and Saturn becomes alive in this Love, a joyous life, giving the properties of their will into Venus; and Venus gives her will to the Sun, and all the life that is born there standeth in true temperance or temperature. But only work thus, and not otherwise, so that Mercury is not angered by his prior opening-up. Outwardly he is evil, but within himself he is good and the true life, but Mars is the cause of life: also, they are not bad in the proper order of opening up. When the unlocking happens in order, the sensual wheel winds around, turning within, until Saturn comes into the inner ground with his will; then he stands in true temperature, and no longer has other inclinations or tendencies.

The philosophical Body is the spiritual Water from the fire and the light, as the Power of the fire and light. When it is separated from coarseness through the unlocking of all the properties of Nature, it is very spiritual. For then the Solar spirit takes no other property into itself but what it may reach into, in the now-open forms of their sensual suns. So the Sun takes nothing into itself but its likeness: It taketh its heaven out of the earth (if you will understand me rightly), for it is its food, from which it gives birth to or generates a young Sun in itself, which is also called Sol; but it is a Body. Thus I say to you, just hold diligently and precisely to this, and you also will rejoice."

How to Practice "Magia" (the Contemplative Philosopher's Stone): According to the Writings of Jacob Boehme, 1575 – 1624.

Jacob Boehme's essential honesty as a seeker compelled him to acknowledge that the employment of language and imagery for accessing Reality is a highly *magical* practice. But he perceived this as an ultimately *transcending,* rather than self-serving, awareness that he associated with the Greek word for wisdom,

"Sophia". It was equally essential for him to delineate the understanding of language and process this conveyed as "Magia", which was *neither* mere mystical musing nor manipulative incantation. It is this concept of "Magia" that we will be considering here, with an eye to specific usages of both language and imagery. Hopefully, it will be understood that this process is a bridge *to eternity,* and a more than adequate facsimile of the same preparation for "crossing over" that Tibetan Buddhists prepare for throughout their lives. As Boehme himself distinguishes, "it is good to have the Noble Stone *of eternity* that gives us assurance by clarifying and pointing out such as were Magi [magicians] *only in history.*"

The Three Stages of Practice:

Substantiality

Like the tarot card of the Sun, with a Child riding in triumph, Boehme reminds us that the school of divine Magia is found in a plain childlike mind. As for the philosophical work of the Stone (Philosopher's Stone), he tells us that *a boy of ten years* might make it. And so we should *behold ourselves* as this boy or girl, holding the cross-wheel ball
of the Stone, which is a three-dimensional rainbow; our hands grasping its blue outer layer, or *substantiality,* with the red radiance of the *fire-glance* in between, and the yellow light of the *eternal liberty and majesty,* around an ever-rotating or pivoting central cross.
It helps of course to connect the *actual matter* of our world with this image; which is why Boehme also remarks that "the philosopher's stone is a very dark, disesteemed stone, of a *grey colour*, but therein lies the highest tincture." Hold *any* stone that has even the slightest

amount of metal or crystal in it, and perceive, with open or closed eyes of wisdom, the sparkle and flash of eternal liberty deep within it. Boehme says: "*Whoever* understands the center of nature, going as far as the light of majesty, is well able to *find* this in the earth and metals. Just learn the correct *entrance,* and the goal is near at hand!" This is like learning to stay on track in the transition between here *and* hereafter, or between matter and the void, in the Tibetan *bardo.* Enter and follow the light to its source, without doubt, without fear, without distraction. There is no more guileless or *childlike* way of doing this than with a stone – *any* stone of your choosing.

The Glance of Fire

The most *famous* single image in Boehme's repertoire, found throughout his writings, is the "morning-redness". This is clearly an evocation of essential *fire* (the middle rainbow band of the red fire-glance). But Boehme wishes us to avoid what he calls the "cold fire" according to the *dark* or harsh impression in our nature that frequently "scorches" us with *false* imaginings. Johann Georg Gichtel, a notable student of Magia as taught by Boehme, explains that these are the kinds of interior assaults that are most *ruinous* of the "gold" within us.

It is for this reason that we evoke the canopy of the *morning-redness* over and around ourselves. It is an effective way of placing ourselves in the light *arising* from divine intention, at the beginning and end of each day. And since the *word* is as important a catalyst as the *image* for achieving awareness in Magia, Boehme's own refrain is especially nice for centering ourselves in that "timeless peace" at the start of each new day: *Now when the dawning or morning-redness shines from east to west, or from rising to setting, assuredly time is no more.* I have also found an effective *complement* to this at day's end or bedtime, in the words of another student of Magia, Johann Conrad Beissel: *Now we shall crown our hope and expectation, since the beautiful evening-redness produces a glimpse of the great day of God that is coming.* Either way, you bring the canopy *over and around* yourself, from east or west, and abide within its peace.

The Eternal Liberty

Boehme reminds us that no creature can exist in fire because "fire consumes the substantiality wherein the natural life stands." But then he points us to the wonderful *paradox* of our human life-form; the fire of our metabolism and digestion, as well as the synapses of our brain, contained in a predominantly *watery* vessel. This is the nature of the living "tincture", arising *out of* the fire and reaching into both the inner and outer bands of the rainbow sphere. While the *outward* oil, the lubricant of substance, holds the shine of life; to *behold* its mystery in ourselves, we must dive or sink deeply *into it.* Boehme says this is not a matter of "hard running" or forced exertion; which is why he resorts to more *fluid* or relaxed verbs here. Yet it does require our *will* or volition; for even to "sink" necessitates our "letting go", an essential *trusting* in divine intention as the source of our life.

We know that we have been met halfway, he says, when "the spirit of the tincture *takes hold of us* and brings us into the *awareness* of eternal liberty," something that cannot be taken away from us again. *This* is the precious Philosopher's Stone, which in accordance with the *aquatic flow* of Boehme's language here, "opens the noble coral wherein we obtain a little pearl." *Put it on,* Boehme says: For it is your "crown of light" that will always illumine the path that you should travel.

■■■

46th *degree,*
Sublime Pastor of the Huts.

Alchemical Diary Entry of the Swedish Behmenist, Erik Eriksson

From a purely Pietistic approach to unlocking Alchemy through "faith and prayer" Eriksson shifts abruptly into sharper, veiled allusions to the seething "Nuclear" Heart of Creation, and the fiery, flowing Gold whose intimate details are possessed by "concealed" Custodians of such Knowledge (reminding this translator of the awesome, if not awful, Catalyst that occurs within a modern Reactor -- how "in growing unctuous or fat, and luxuriant, it increases and spreads itself forth infinitely in power."Aurora 22: 101)*

*See the Meditation, "Holocaust of Regeneration," immediately following the translation of Eriksson below. RR

Dated Feb. 22, 1756: Addressed to my dear confidant Wän.

A Chymical Faith Confession, dealing primarily with my opinion on the Gold Tincture. A short description where I reflect upon the way of the Heavenly Pearl-Stone and concealed treasure; which is Christus in the entire Fulness of his eternal and adopted Manhood. The outcome of God's fiery judgments, is the pleasant and beautiful Lily-Time, when the Sons of God will pass through to Summer by means of Wisdom's lush greenness. For when the weeds, thistles, thorns and all seedlings that prevented God's Work are uprooted by the roots and burned, then breaks forth the Deity's Lily-League in its right Depth, Height, Length, and Breadth.   The entrance to the veritable wealth which is hidden from this grieving earth, and consists of fine gold, Bedolah and Soham, or the vaunted Stone of the Wise (Genesis 2: 11, 12), shall be a victorious Faith, a Cross of Fruit-Bearing Virtues, God's Love and Righteousness through Christum Jesum.

Yes, the *ability* that will make gold is frequent praying beneath the Cross: *this* it is that discovers the First Matter; that also reveals the occult or hidden learning, how visible things are generated out of the invisible, how out of transparent Brightness, golden Glory, and the highest degree of Purity, the power of Spirit transforms Mercurium. *Following* Holy Spirit's declaration, His immutable element, located *in* the united Vegetable, Animal and Mineral mass, is the New Man's Hammer and Golden Key, and breaks the hard Iron Bars of Nature with which the Treasury is sealed. God that *giveth* the applicants judgment according to their own faith, also bestows *power* to all by faith in God; so right praying will again *see* a renewed Saturnum shine in Jovial Properties, Mars likewise out of the new Venus, and Mercurium shine in Silver with the Lunar spirit; and Jovem with Luna and Venus out of the Solar Kingdom, the Sun's essence being located *in* the Elemental Kingdom. Thus may our Mercurius, Lead, Tin, Iron, Copper, Silver and Gold be transmuted out of fiery, fine, flowing heavenly Gold which stands in everlasting Eternity. *Such* is now the order of the decreasing and increasing Degrees of the Planets. There remains then for the sake of how to *purify* the foundation, the significance of the 12 characters or signs, and all 12 of Jerusalem's foundations.

Thus Aries represents the Lamb of God's Regiment in Nature, Taurus, even the Independence of Wisdom Herself, Gemini, Love, Fertility; Cancer, a Hiding Place, and Kindness in the Good; Leo, a Conquering and Winning over Strength; Virgo, the Purity of all Deeds; the Scales, Righteousness in all Dealings; Scorpion, Chastity in all Friendship; Sagittarius, a Convenient Community of All of God's Ways; Capricorn, Freedom from all Evil; Aquarius, Boldness in all Phenomena; Pisces, Exemption from Evil, as well as all Horrors. Now to say with a few words, and with the *consent* of the unified ancient Wise Ones themselves, how that correct Universal Aurum potabile, or fine, fiery Liquid Gold out of the Spiritual Sun is the highest total power of the rest of the Planets:

Wherefore, since the Golden Tincture dissolves and transforms the purified metals, also drives the dead body from their midst; would not God's Son with his *Divinely*-instituted Tincture and fiery Gold of Love, be able to accomplish man's whole transformation from the midst of a carnal state, in *accordance* with that Spirit? Let the whole world *alone* that wants to contest the truth and become unfaithful; so long as you, however, *cherish* God's faithfulness; indisputably fixed in the availability of Jesu Christi's Love-Gold, Divine Aurum potabile or Holy Breath, as an all-transforming Mercurius, capable of tinging and restoring the entire nature of mankind, so that the dead body shall be *like* his transfigured Body, sheer Gold-Flaming Majestic Glory, valued more than gold, and more precious than the fine gold of Ophir. *Nothing* having an eternal Basis, in Nature and the Great World's Creation, through all the Cycles of Time, and then in St. John's Revelation -- according to our Magic Fire-Magnet, called the *Baculus Jacobi* or Jacob's Staff – seems difficult at all to us! Which things, however, are *only* felt and diligently kept by worthy *God*-wise men, who are themselves conditioned by the higher Magic and supernatural Sciences, of which especially the high Society of Rosencreutz possesses a large Inventory. (But praise God that He hath *hidden* the high and wise *from* the ignorant.) If it could become *aware* of the effects of our Fire-Glass and Air-Magnet, the world would certainly be amazed and horrified: It would not *nearly* be able to comprehend what a fiery nature our Azoth and Sigillum Hermetis hath; and in what way, shining Diana *transforms* this into a ruby-red Oil with the spiritually-resistant Gold and brimstone of Fire! [*Translator's* note: the diary entry and discussion of Alchemy breaks off at this point.]

****

The Holocaust of Regeneration

In aspiring to the birth of our light-being, it's highly unlikely we will ever *glow*, if we haven't first passed through nature's *fire;* and that requires a property or quality that is described in the literature as 'majesty' – consider it as something that rules 'naturally' without the need for force.

It is rather like the twelve-story Olympic-size *pool* that contains a nuclear reactor's rods in all of their potency. L.C. de Saint-Martin and Boehme speak of the 'refrigeration' of Lucifer's *original* holocaust, as a radical cool-down that still reflected the residual light remaining, with the brilliancy of a sunlit iceberg. However, it first necessitated the plunging or 'descent' of nature's unleashed, *lethal* urges into a containment field.

Here is where we must grasp the implied meaning of the 'mystical death', which in aspiring to regeneration, is *our own.* In other words, we *too* must sink 'twelve-stories down'— if our innate antagonism to enlightenment requires such a drowning. And then we will no longer need to *fear* our residual, natural 'uranium glow'. For it will be clear to us that it is safely *contained* in the majestic and divine serenity provided for this: the Abyss called Love.

****

GOLD FROM MIDNIGHT: A Thorough Description of the Supreme Jewel of the World, by Johann Philip Maul (1714): English translation by Russell Yoder; with additional illuminations from De Roode Leeuw, of Goossen van Vreeswijk.

Johann Philipp Maul (1662-1727), a Swiss-born physician educated at Heidelberg and Leiden, used his fascination with the healing properties of local mineral springs, as the 'springboard' for advocating a reconciliation of matter and spirit grounded in Hermetic therapy. His voluminous writings, from which the following compilation has been extracted, are originally in the form of conversations ("table talk") on living the life of a Chymist: providing, in essence, a clear prescription for meditating upon the transformational processes which comprise a divinely-generated Creation. Rather uniquely, he takes the Book of Job as his initial model.

Midnight Chaos Profoundly see whilst probing the depths.

Midday Gold — Joy-Realm of Venus The Celestial and Golden Rain of the Water Above: It is the

Center of Nature.

The study of Chymie is the Contemplation of Life Essences, a Meditative discipline that takes Life as it truly IS, and

resolves all uncharitable wranglings of dogma and contrived disputations of Man in the Alembic of daily devotion; implementing always a hands-on approach to unraveling the Godly Mysteries of Matter that lead back to Spirit. Amongst others, the Wondrous Author of our times, Jacob Böhme, says that Chymie delivered him from contentious Religion and dispute. So we have taken from the same man, this view in everything: For, without knowledge of Chymie, nothing can be assessed in-depth.

****

Commentary on the Copper-Plates Preceding the Title- Page:

Christian, look at the Cross on both sides! To capture the Gold from Midnight Black, you have to go hand in hand with Black [in the Scripture so often named Zalmavath, or the shadow of death; compare with Job 18: 4]. Your eye must see Black; Fontani of Sulfur-Fire [consisting of and corresponding with the juice-running Blackberry Bush in Sinai, burning and not burning in the vacant or Empty Fire, signifying tribulation and recovery].

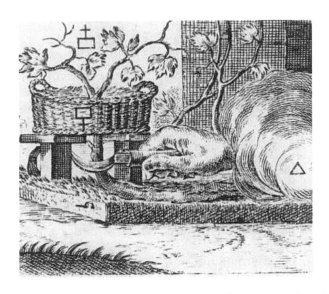

So out of the Midday Light cometh Fontina Bernhardina [incoming Rachamin to Cabbalists, or Aqueous-Living Bounty; and Böhmen's Joy-Realm], called refined or noble Gold of Faith: HOD [is the word, as it standeth in our text: the Praise, Honor, Majesty which cometh with the Joy-Realm, in the Cabbala], by Gloria Trina!

Yes Indeed! Zaphon's mountain ranges are terrible to penetrate! [Therefore Zaphon, meaning midnight and hidden treasures (as the text of Job 37: 22 says), thus lies in hard and unsightly mountains of stone.]

But it cannot be otherwise if you want to be a successful human being! [Enosh (Job 28: 4), a poor decayed 'black' man, could nevertheless move the waters, as well as the heavens and the earth!]

Thou canst devise the Treasure by Salt [particularly the rock salt, ignited in the anger, impatience, and rashness that is not gracious there], Sulfur [that indeed makes the spirit flowing in heat, but not burning in vain lust], Steam [so that the stinking natural dry vapor or smoke of sins is dampened and suppressed; and on the other hand transformed into a healthy absorbing water, called Ignis voporosus, and Fontina Bernhardina, or Ignis Nubium, and the same everlasting faith-fire] and Heat, which you need to overcome, seated in the depths of Humility [through the Tartarum, after which figure in a Salt-earth, as indicated by the Philosophers, you have Salt (namely, the Wisdom in you that is there in Humility)].

God Himself dwelleth in the Dark! [Psalm 97: 2; Psalm 18: 6, 12]. A Fire goeth before Him. [Psalm 97: 3].

In the Weather He speaks [Job 38: 1 & 40, 1; it. Job 37: 21] to JOB [HIOB is a true historical figure who amidst trials of decay redeems the world: and in like manner the Chymical matter, together with the same operations that it must pass through, particularly in the Blackness testing its resolution, goeth forth from this afterwards as Gold. Job 23: 10.] saying that He dwelleth in the Darkness [2 Chronicles 6: 1].

Therefore do not shy away from the Terrible, for the Majesty will glisten, and show your God shining in the Dark Cross. [There is a glossy Blackness then, because of the conserved and increased spiritual or Mercurial substrate- Humidity, or Moisture content.]

You go from the Left Hand [The Left signifies in the Cabbala Midnight or the place of Judgment, where the Black Cross stands erect. Therefore Heaven, above the Christian world, is at Golgotha; which Cross through Galgal, branches environmentally to the Right or Midday, and is depressed, praecipitated, swallowed up in a Figure of Gold, and thus transformed into the Joy-Realm, or Venus of Wisdom.] continually to Zion; [even as Christ arriving from his journey out of Galilee by the Sea Chinnereth (Sea of Galilee), and teaching 'Zion'—the city of Jerusalem lying at Midnight, in which Source Golgotha and Galgal are.

The Sea Chinnereth or Galilee (in the Cabbala, the Green, namely representing the inward-colored Vitriol of the Land itself), runs along the Jordan, which is the adjoining significant character, through the Salt-Sea, under the Earth Cabbalistice, into the Red Sea; and therefore—conciliated and preserved from Fire—awakens and brings the Air-Water or the Golden Rain.]

To the Center of Nature Go! The Luminous Spot of the Cross, Bright as the Risen Sun now Show! Joy-Realm's Cross, quenching without Fire, Slakes your thirst and Stills your Desire!

Gold comes from Midnight [It is the Cross, humility, humiliation, reversal, rebirth; "I'm black," says David (Psalm 38: 7 basic text) "throughout the day, namely my life"; particularly when it comes to the smelting or melting and crucifixion of the old Adam; which, because it is a true deliquescence (Psalm 22: 15; Job 10: 10; Ezekiel 22: 22; Malachi 3: 3; Psalm 97: 5; Psalm 147: 18; Psalm 86: 10 and many similar ones), is flowing through everywhere, as the good Ground-Moisture with Love, without

which True Solution or Melting of Love within the breast, the entire Christendom is truly only loud hypocrisy and heresy.] to praise the great God, Who brings Gold out of the dust (4 Esdras 8: 2; Job 28: 6) and Life out of death. [Therefore, in accordance with the significance of the crushing or contrition of dust; which, although according to the presentation in Ezra, is little enough, still is necessary, as without it everything other than the prescribed Gold of Faith is merely Sophistry or the powdered stuff of the Imagination.]

Which Life exists in vita vegetabili, animali & rationali [and therefore in all three considerations of the Human Soul, as: 1) Nephesch (growth of the sensitivity of the Heart); 2) Ruach (movement of the life-spirits in the affections, especially of Love) wherein the act of Faith has its true Hypostasis or Essence of Being (Galatians 5: 5; Hebrews 11: 5); and 3) Neschamah (the exercise of Reason)].

****

Spiritual truth is itself in and of Nature, and all corporeal works as they are made and ordered by God; linked and thus indissolubly connected. However, perhaps the most illuminating examples of the foremost works of God in all of Nature (Job 40: 14) are the terrible Behemoth, and the cruel King over all the Children of the Black Lion (Job 41: 25), the Leviathan; which are quite beyond our gaze and comprehension, just as our Gold from Midnight is—simply to prove to ourselves that IT can be MADE! And as the Title of our Discourse is the Gold from Midnight (rather than

Midday, as with Guinea, Peru, etc.) this will accord for the better part with that of Midnight as North; because the North is composed of hard, rocky, magnetic and iron-adhering subterranean mountains which come from the dark, black depths of the earth, and at last principally from the cold black digestion of the magnetic Midnight-rock of Zaphon.

Concerning the Gold of Midnight, or the Supreme Medicine

The Fama of the Rosicrucians calleth gold the cursed aurificium, when it is regarded otherwise than as a consequence of added Wisdom; a barley-grain's weight of the same (as well as of Zaphon, Midnight's treasure), being worth well over half a ton of such treasure! But what grounds have we to complain? The time of the Sea of Glass is not yet finished, and Sophia is not yet reigning over Pluto.

However, because Nature is made for the sake of the Spiritual, not the Spiritual made for the bodily nature's sake, it follows that the bodily must accommodate itself in accordance with the Spiritual; and the visible is the mirror of the invisible. Although, the strongest proof is clearly furnished from the basic Hebrew texts, for now I just want to talk simply of crude Minerva, and about the procreations of the metals; but nevertheless, about their secret conception (not as a fool, or as a gardener saying he is making salad merely by sowing and planting).

It is prudent to ponder that metals are all made of matter just as are people. Matter is terrestrial, as earth and water, and celestial as Aether of the Sun (thus also man). Corporeal nature's spirit reflects the incorporeal mind of the Spiritual World. Matter is made mutable; and who would thus argue that God does not have the power to create (therefore, man)? The change, however, is within the body, if already darkened by corporeal impurity; not in the spirit, the spiritual elements, or the clear light.

The defilement of the metals occurs through the non-shining poison and earthly mixture: that of humans, through the darkening of the mind (the poison of Satan) and earthly sense-awareness. However the improvement of metals occurs in the earth through the Solar Aether (the substantial gilding solar-power), where they are planted instead as completely Solar seeds by the Mercurial Water. This gilding Solar power or Blessed Solar Seed constitutes a hearty welcome from Christ: Hion (Job) calleth it "Goel," a deleteria venenositate to the metallic seed in the Archetype (or Original). It is also in typography, "Shekinah" to the Chymical Rabbis; to the heathen poets, "Perseus"; to Chymici (chemists) "Hercules," or the Glory of the Air (Aeris Gloria)—that is, "Samson" (from the Sun).

This Solar Aether comes from heaven, but is born physically in the metals, even at the same time it regenerates the same into their right golden seeds and Principio. Iron is the least of the metals, but the most useful in Mechanics, and **C**hemistry (when ordinary); although not in the "Natural" worthiness of its **N**ature. It depicts the **C**ross and suffering, whereby regeneration is promoted: it even gives it, but not its validity, which results from the Shekinah. As in the dispute of the Philosopher with the Knight of War over the common gold, the victory was awarded **"to iron";** however his "red flowers" were ordered to be lent to the **M**onarchy of the metals, but only as a duty to Shekinah. Iron and Shekinah are close relatives, which proves the material is striated (materia striata), and all metals are born of **I**ron. Consequently each one can redound to perfection, when earnestly requested;

and to a durable, resistant state of calm that is believed to be correct.

Other than for its true Chymical preparation, Iron has less supple and soft figure-forming sulfur, than Cyprian copper; but for this lesser alkaline salt to be divided, it loves Mercurius for its cleansing first. Thus, although not everyone has everything, all can reach perfection when each earnestly uses metals such as this one for the common good. Then they would already increase more and more, by the Gradus and Carrathas, and through the 10th Sephira's Sphere: **So** Sublimate *the Celestial* until it comes to the Empyrean Astro-Sun. Who then is faithful in little, is placed over many.

He that is not stupefied by water and fire, by the challenge of salniter and sulfur of tartar, penetrates the great Emblem of the Wonder-World (equal to the gold of the North from Midnight, Job 19: 3) like Hiob (Job); through the 10th Chymical "process of calumnies," driven as the spiritual **G**old of our fountain, from the underground fire, through the waters rising to the heights, on purely shining wings, as the proof of a pure and healthy potion of which he is a partaker through the Solar Aether. Then, while this golden sunshine is present throughout nature—though not visible, yet in its operative power—so it gives itself only to those who are proper, to enjoy with benefits for which it is convenient and worthy; that is, lodged in the place prepared by God.

All matter of the sea, by the continually-circulating alteration of its parts which is sufficient for all earth**ly** creatures, and also for human bodies, simply follows the figure and capacity its matter receiveth from the heavens; the forms or souls (thus, not by traducem, but also not freshly-made; from the **C**reation of the world on the **f**irst **d**ay); just as, in fact, with man's so-called spiritual "**S**oul." Not all the matter in the sea that is rushing in the depths of the earth, is for **G**old, I say; but that which is the very least amount of all; not for lack of the Solar Aetheris or Sulphuris, but because the other parts do not accept it!

Much of it is for toxic smoke over the iron crust of the subterranean fire, the **great** quantity of people in the fire of the Cross; stones much too hard! Many too are half- metals and minerals; finally, some partly for metals which are to be **G**old, when the externals do not prevent this: for this cause simply to create all **who are** capable, who**m** the **S**pirit is already purifying, maturing, and figuring. Then, with whom they sensibly unite**,** by taking **their** shape from them, they remain in heavenly love; the same as those who persevere unto the end, proving that they are rightly figured and sealed.

Because these parables are without end in this world, it is only needful to report that **G**old, rather than the lesser metals, was created in such perfection; that its perfect sulfur, or Soham, and pure single mercury, or Bedolah was at hand (Genesis 2: 12). But this was in a state of innocence. Keeping track of **gold coming directly from the earth** is not quite so savory! Rather, everything growing is passing through its gradus of impurity. The water itself must be separated and made clean for subtle beauty, when it will constitute **nutrition** and a living spirit.

Which reminds us of our **own** nutrition: While diet is the same as the health of the body, since every one, as his own physician, can remember to satisfy his nature with less, before the latter stages of life; **S**ouls which are not satisfied with less, but rather require **A**ll that is (i.e. God), have their health from Wisdom. It is wondrous then, that the body **which** is overloaded dwindles, namely, since the food does **not** truly please; while "Chymice" are exalted as if truly in paradise! However, the **S**oul shall never be so sated with its food of Wisdom, that it is overloaded; but the more it

enjoys thereof the more gleeful it is.

Wondrous, nevertheless, that in the Holy Scriptures which themselves make so much of the workings of silver, gold, and metals, one reads nothing of their **C**reation, as well as **that** of the angels. These are commemorated with such **things** as were **made of the** Tohu and Bohu, the Chaos or "**P**rima **M**ateria," from which the Light was called and created on the first Day. For the **G**old as well as its associated Soham and Bedolah was already thought of in paradise, as a composite molten-Light of the Sun, just as the Sun itself is an ever-fiery molten nugget of **G**old.

This gilding, golden Aether of the Sun, or substantial Light, of which everything under the Sun—up to and including Saturnum—is governed and enlightened, spreadeth throughout the world; being the nearest tool in the life-spirit of our Soul, and of the angels in their appearance and bodily action. Ever redder is the blood and ever-healing, the more of this Light there is in the life-spirits; and the more sanguine and cheerful is the man! For the Light expands the mind, and so does the Soul in propagating its thoughts merrily, which nonetheless happens because the Light has more of the life-spirits in the blood, as its right seat.

However, the intelligent have glowing life-spirits, because they disconnect from the crude through meditation. Therefore as the light is drawn in continually with the air, a wise man is made cheerful; and that's why you need to breathe 100 times in an hour. Now the Scripture says (Hebrews 11: 2), that all those worlds (Olamoth, Aeon) that are—the Subterranean, the Terrestrial, and so many Celestial bodies with their Vorticibus or upheavals, have been completed through God's Word; not from what appeareth, which is visible. That is, (1) the world is not eternal; always a visible comes from another visible; however, (2) that out of which all visible things arise is invisible, because this Total Force is the "Fundamental-Text."

But what about the invisible, and consequently smaller and more subtle bodies, such as the **L**ight, together with its several hundred parts which are not seen? Lastly, we must consider that the Metallic beginnings are also the initial beginnings of all other visible things. For they are very agile and subtle, and therefore invisible (unless there is a good deal more that is clotted together). How then can that which is not seen in our **sour spring- or well-water** become dissipated itself, by distillation, into its simple particles? (Mercurius, quo omnia metalla constant, aut totus avolat, aut totus manet in igne.)

So although it's not designated on which **D**ay the metals and the angels were actually created, they are indisputably there **in the Text!** Indeed the Wise (to whom God gives enlightened eyes of the mind) can see more embedded in Scripture than most. But for the Spirits inhabiting the high levels, it is not necessary for them to be any place to have their impact or effect, even without ethereal spatial tools. And we cannot commemorate God majestically enough!

Nevertheless, all creatures, and all the host of heaven, have such a close relationship among themselves, and towards humans, as to be ruled by the same species of Solar Aetheris; otherwise they could not compose its connexion, correspondence, and sympathy. And therefore the Highest Medicine of the people on this earth, and their sympathy with all the other heavens and those creatures which are in **them**, is because of only one Saviour (created to represent the same), not only the present enterprises, but all Superior worlds.

Even their own breath is nothing but a sympathy of their lives with the Sun and the Stars; quite analogous in its own right to the sympathies of two blood-friends, one of whom is suffering on the Danube of an infectious fever, the cause of which is that the other on the Rhine is infected at the same time! Just consider how Rhenish vines in England know precisely when the vines bloom in Germany.

To offer you one telling example of the mysterious workings of such sympathy, among others I have encountered (far removed from both superstition and gullibility): A gentlewoman was dangerously ill, at precisely the time that one of her friends, living 40 miles from her abode, passed away. At night, in the parlor where the lady

reposed, a knocking was heard 3 or 4 times, one after the other, which also occurred quite a few times the following night.

I was summoned to the patient because of this knocking, which I was curious to hear. I was not in her room long, when there was a knock three times in succession, as when the pulse, in a fever, beats strongly in order; brightly, in the air, such that one could not distinguish whether the sounds were against the top of the rafters, or against the wall where the patient happened to be lying.

But I could tell it was intended more against the wall, and at the height of the large room. I knocked on the wall, opened and visited within all of the doors (whereof in doing so I was astonished, because there was nothing). It was after midnight; yet we had a good conscience, and nothing to fear, such as of a lively ghost from evil people who are not at peace. Nowhere could I find any cause that would ideally create a likeness of this knocking.

As I correctly specified the medicine for the patient to take, there was a knock again 4 times, loud and hard, as I said, in the air; which afterwards was heard on the following nights (as I was told), and more times, additionally, until the threat of death in this patient was over and gone. I doubt not that these things took place through an inclined sympathy of the aether (corrupted equally in her blood and that of her friend) as a "copulam explosivam" constituted of salniter and sulfur, dampening the bloodstream.

For I also have a patient who is struggling well into the sixth year from the otherwise rare disease, diabetes; where all of the body attracteth so much salnitric moisture from the air into itself quite often; especially at night, because the air is more salnitric than during the day. At certain times, when not prevented by medicine, the "copula explosiva" gives rise to epileptic seizure; out of the source of the unified salniter and sulfur, with a precipitated salt of ashes (from which there is much to deduce in medicine and Chymie). Note: Medical practitioners today may disagree; but nevertheless, this is a curious testimony to the comparative rarity of diabetes, in an age far less reliant upon sugar as a dietary staple than ours!

Now I suppose that in the above example, the sympathetic salnitric aether can move from dampening into an "explosionem elasticam," and the coiled vapors burst in the blood, after the likeness of a little thunder (as travel descriptions often report and maintain to happen from the salnitric air of the Nile); causing such a loud knocking proportionally, according to the pulse or anxious palpitation; and indeed, high in the air towards the bed, where it resounds against the ceiling and the walls; and at last with good reason!

For whenever such portions have not sufficiently evaporated, but rather been drawn into oneself (the body, and particularly, the lungs, thereby developing a strong asthma and cough); then it will be such a corruption of the blood, as with her and her friend, thus creating the risk of death.

Otherwise, when such a poltergeisting "clatter" arises in houses and has hidden, but natural causes, it comes from a common union of mineral or metallic vapors of the earth, coupled with heavy air, and such a "clang" as happens to be the cause because of the location, as when kettles fall: or as in the Balkans, where a load of buried metal was dropped into the ground, it can be drawn forth again, by sympathy, through the penetrating subsurface metallic vapors; even more so when it lies concealed around someone dead or murdered, because all the vapors interact so powerfully.

When, together with Paracelsus, we perceive the true **P**hilosophy of **N**ature well enough to be directed from reason and Scripture, we have more certainty in speaking of it, and no need of peculiar, sensible, but mortal ghosts.

This is least certain, however, where the metallic vapors, or Spiritus seminales aurei—the seminal spirits of **G**old—are; because these must be imagined by us, from their certain texture and context, since we cannot plumb what is without any shape or form, without dispersing or filling with smoke all that is there, as well as the wonderful Sympathy that emerges as intended vapors, when it is pure and made subtle; just such a matter as the *L*ight of the Sun has spread or propagated through the whole world, whereby the most wonderful effects of **N**ature occur.

For me, then, the golden arrow Albarea—"light, not heavy"—of **Pythagoras,** and the wonderful Stone of the Indian Thuano (as Methosius alleges) no doubt consisted of such matter! This Stone sparkled like the bright **S**un beaming, and gleamed into his eyes, so that it was almost not to be endured. While it could not *lie* down upon the earth, yet it was laid low, but constantly in the open air, and floating in it, since it was nothing but fire. Note: Without delving into further examples of this, suffice it to say such reports are commonplace in the various Indian siddha-traditions.

For though it already consisted of metal, it was separated into pure **L**ight, and thus heavy and light at the same time when it arose into or out of its Centre; because—although nothing is more difficult than the configuring of **L**ight— also nothing comes about more easily than divided **L**ight. In a word, the Stone was so highly exalted through the multiplication of fire, that it was equal to the **S**un, as was already reported above; in that **G**old and the **S**un are all the same matter.

Finally, along these lines, I wish to employ an experiment I learned, that is also a fine medicine: When you have a good Regulum stellatum (starry Regulus) make it a pure powder, and set it well-sealed in hot sand. Such will then be glittering white-light, of 10 to 11 ounces. Purge it no longer; for you can medically configure the powdered Algoreth from it!

It is only the fire and heat that causes this stuff to be hard: the greatest work of the fiery **L**ight is in readily and easily making one merry, in precisely the same way as the healthy and enlightening life-spirits of people who are skipping and dancing, either with their body**,** or **even merely** in the mind.

Although there are bodies, which make the **L**ight harder, for example, **T**in, which—exalted in solem (the **S**un)—is harder than before; that cometh, as I said above, because the **L**ight is configured, so that it would easily be brought into the highest **M**ultiplication and heavenly nature. As for the renowned Bergmännlein (mountain dwarves), reported by so many, their matter is a harder, rich, metallic haze, having a lot of immature quicksilver in it. But whether other spirits are also clothed in **this**, I let be for now.

Understand that truth, science, and knowledge, are food of the **S**oul, and distinguish us from beasts who seek primarily to eat and drink for the belly. What God does through his created **N**ature, he wants to be noted by his creatures! So if a person—together with Thales—at all times contains life, not only will he have fun, but also sojourn healthily, hand in hand with both **B**ody and **S**oul.

THE
POTABLE GOLD OF THE ANCIENTS:

Original Verses by Gerard of Cremona (1250)

Together with A Concise Anonymous Commentary,

As Translated from the French

****

Though Thrace has its part, that is rich in gold and Orpheus
(Thrace, land of Mars where—according to Orpheus—the mystery
of the Cabiri that the Phoenicians introduced and made famous,
was popular),

Yet the trophy herein is in another spreading river.
At the hidden center of Mother Nature, the indicator of Two
Vapors (these vapors follow one after the other; one white and
the other yellow, as Nature will lead you to form these subjects),

I quit with pleasure the writing of other authors,
And do not want at all what they inform me of!

Annotation:

These two are two Spirit Vapors containing the four elements,
which we must deeply consider the source and origin of all
Nature, because those who do will have the true knowledge. Who
does not know the true qualities and virtues will remain always
ignorant both of works, and all natural substances in the world,
as the Philosopher said: "they wander, they wandered, they will
wander; because such philosophers have not produced the
proper agent, the most comfortable and shortest path; thus
leaving all sophisticated books and focusing the mind, to consider
the effects of Nature.

I begin, and I see the center of the earth by the burning heat of
the radiant sun; these Two Spirits going forth, and waging war,
producing flashes and lightning in my eyes.

Annotation:

There is great sympathy and correspondence between the
spherical sun and the central sun, and that is what Hermes says
at the beginning of his Emerald Tablet, because what is above is
like what is below, to perpetrate the miracles of only One thing;
because we see that the sun draws to itself its very nature—
vapors and humidity of the earth, like dew and mist, or dense
fumes—and leading both upward they have their natural meeting
place which is air: and these vapors form into clouds, wherein

the water, heavy and viscous, is forced to fall back to its center which is the land, where itopens pores, and in this way causes here steam or a hot exhalation that, drawn by the heat of the sun in a cold region of the air, occasions the thunder and lightning.

And then in various ways—whether as dew or frost—by mutual consent, redoubling their more-than-perfect effect over terrestrial places.

Annotation:

Philosophers have referred to this up and down movement as sublimation, because, in this action, subtle things are made massive and dense, and bodily ones are made lighter and subtle; and therefore such different kinds of spirit, after being at war with each other for a long time, accord with each other over time, and are friends; joining closely together, flying in the air and then falling together to earth, which causes the descent ~ a philosophical dew which nourishes our land, and maketh it bring forth and bear a twofold fruit as a result.

And also the same man who is forever at war, although he is only the sovereign of all animals.

Annotation:

So here we truly produce with this dew or liquor, as we acknowledge Mother Nature with her workers—and, amongst others—which her servant Archse takes such pains to teach us, & discover the route and path prepared and maintained in all Her works and operations; as without artifice She works in a single manner, a single substance in one vessel, and yet creates & produces various things from a unique material, that philosophers have called Chaos of the said first-two Vapors or Spirits; whose qualities are one active and the other passive.

The earth is nourished and all that it embraces,

Plants, animals, marcasites, metals,
So curious, and filled with joy,
I scrap the work formerly suffered by me
And would approach my mistress Nature more closely,
Requesting the gifts that She has offered me.

Annotation:
The artist after admitting his previous ignorance that blinded him to his faults, welcomes what comes in the light and knowledge of Nature, requests Her to show him the foundation of this medicine, and the subject which causes and generates the birth of this medicine as admirable, & desirest what She grants to him for the composition and operation of that in which he has so often erred, as he says:

She at once, listening to my prayer,
Unsealed my eyes that had been open to nothing,
And opening the customary door or gate of these places,
(beginning with putrefaction), She said:
Well, here are my treasures discovered!

Annotation:

O Nature, how sweetly thou watchest; benignly and promptly to rescue the sons of science by pulling them out of the abyss and dark caves of ignorance in which they were engaged, and as a natural Mother you deign to give of thy partially open bosom and breasts to show us what you hold most dear and precious; and then thy liberal hand givest us more than we deserve, because you unseal our eyes, revealing to us the true male and female matter that produces and engenders our medicine which, once recognized, we are surely able to work!

Nature, in my prayers, permits me to see them.
I know about the first origin of these spirits,
I recognize their effect, strength and power,
Even though, as spirits, they are stripped of form.

Annotation:

This is the perilous passage in which many learned operators, who have been misled and misguided by such matter, take strange materials, the male for the female agent, the dry for the wet patient, water for fire. These spirits are all still wearing their terrestrial and dark dress, so it is almost impossible for a man to be able to know and see. But after being washed and stripped of impurities, and original and superfluous stains, we can know the incontinent (which dissolves in spirit), & take from them what is necessary to perform and compose the magisterium.

I take and enclose them, in equal measure
Inside the egg of a massive crystal, clear and shiny.
Then my Art, assisting Nature's
Sunlight (central)—or Sulphur (also understood to mean the sun, the fire of the Athanor); — I am going to cook everything.

Annotation:
This combination is necessary because it is the first way and composition of our solvent water called mercurial and where it leads, as it is that which makes the separation and dissolution of the adjacent parts, and is named for the effect of the Mercury of mercury, as the wise man says:

"This is indeed a simple mineral water which comes to water the earth so that it germinates and bears fruit in due time."

Latin: "For it is the water of the dew of May: she washes and whitewashes the bodies of the rain anew, as it were, and makes a new body from two bodies." [French: This is a dew of springtime in May (or rather Maie) who washes and whitens the body as much as she penetrates, and indeed makes a new one of two bodies.]

O How precious and beautiful is this water; she is named the Philosophers' water and soul of the dissolved substances, without which our medicine and work cannot achieve success and perfection, thus:

I admire the effect and the red color.
First the compost dissolves in clear water
Slackens its power and rich greenness,

And worldly power is born of these two.

Annotation:

This water is truly a virtue and a wonderful power over what is its nature (because it rots by degrees), showing all of a sudden its action upon matters that are pleasing to it, and like a miracle & masterpiece, it dissolves &liquefies solids; and by making the perfect incombustible oil and permanent penetrating dye, is full well what the Philosopher claims, saying:

Latin: "Our water immediately dissolves the gold and silver, and the incombustible oil does that which can then be mixed with other imperfect bodies." [French: Therefore our water dissolves gold and silver on the spot, and is the incombustible oil, which can then be mixed with other imperfect bodies].

These bodies are dissolved, and thus called quicksilver and the menstrual—which is not without its sulphur or salt-accompanied luminaries we usually call the sun and moon, that are the main means by which Nature goes about refining and accomplishing the generation & finishing the work.

I remain joyful, and no longer ask to be in heaven.
And I thank God for the end of work,
the whole jubilant summit,
Casting care and sadness away from me.

Annotation:

The philosopher having finished perfecting the medicine no longer desires the rest, being very pleased with God and Nature to have such a reward, the end of his work, and does not care about the world or even anything that depends upon it; and Hermes says about him: He will have the glory of the world and all obscurity will be removed from before his eyes, that is to say, all ignorance and poverty & disease: having recognized what comes from such medicine, virtue and power, he can only think of enjoying the eternal bliss of heaven as soon as possible. However, compassionately, he wishes to teach his former brothers, and pull them out of error; and speaking to the ignorant of this Art he says to them:

Neither have ye regrets, in breaking all of your vessels!

Poor blind people, who are driven by avarice,
Looking for no rest without the hermetic secret;
Seeing this spirit in your mind, leave all artifice behind,

Annotation:
And certainly with good reason we can see how there are people ignorant of all solar Mineral and Metallic root- sources of Nature, whom no theory or practice or knowledge—while working blindfolded thereunto at full speed—brings to the object and perfection of our work and so-laudable medicine; who simply read a book or two full of false recipes, that such authors have made for misuse and the unlearned in this Art; which perpetrators, not having been able or known how to reach the goal of their desires, have written & slandered the elders who possessed the liquor and powder as estimated; and instead of listening to the sayings and
writings of the ancients, have taken their most common and familiar drugs—talc, common salt, alum, vitriol, arsenics, réalgars—sublimated and other substances of everything foreign and hostile to our work and nature; and subsequently have wanted to imagine that with such drugs they will draw forth or derive mercury, and in this way increase the perfect metal!

Puffing is not the purpose of the wise philosopher Sublime, calcine, dissolve, congeal
Your poisons are not the subject of the work
Quit all such, and we can better speak.

Annotation:
If those who are inquisitive & lovers of this noble Science, well understood and intended, say all the writings of ancient Sages who tell unanimously that the matter of this philosophical powder is common and universal, although not known; what is of Science & virtually everywhere, in every house, should it fall into the hands of all people and be sold at a low price so that the poor could have as much as the wealthiest, and the practice and the work be so easy that a simple woman, without turning away from her customary tasks, could be led to perfection, they would be fully satisfied!

One mercury is sufficient but it is one of the wise, Who is hiding in it a life to be accomplished.
It is fickle, as it has a watery image,
A vessel of two stars, being full and empty.

Annotation:
In truth, the substance of mercury, whereof our medicine is made, is enclosed and imprisoned in the body of our magnesia; but those who know him very well extract it within a short time, and pull it out of the womb of our lion by force, and through our solvent or water (heretofore so frequently alleged), and which is nothing but a white vapor—fluid—however, not wetting the hands.

Latin: "And it is the smoke that nourisheth white gold." [French: The white vapor is the white gold.]

This is therefore the firstborn body of the Spirit of Nature, that contains in itself the four elements which just form around the water the Philosophers have nominated Pontic water, which has such a form and feel that is pleasing to the Artist (as included in the following preparation):

One of these Two Spirits taken pure from his land
Gently dissolves through a vaporous low heat;
And another that encircles his belly by the joint
Through the effect of a soft love embrace.

Annotation:
Herein is the point, that it is necessary to have intelligence specifically so as not to be deceived in the composition of our true medicine because, as I said heretofore, everything that multiplies needs conjunction of our male and female matter, which is known only to those of the Art; but there are two others who are mediators of said materials, however, acting as opposites, one extremely hot and dry, which is called agent, and the other cold and damp, named patient; but following preparation, they wish for conjunction and marriage, joining and embracing tenderly and sointimately together, until they are made an inseparable substance, such that what was fire and water, is water having fire; which water is the Philosophical mercury, and the fire is called the Philosophers' sulphur.

The natural sulphur around everything of mercury

Sublimates and—gently cooking—stops
The living poison from incessantly festering,
In order to serve as a true medicine of the body.

Annotation:
As Hermes, Father of Philosophers, aptly said and argued in his short discourse, and amply spoke of the natural qualities of our medicine; saying our work contains within itself the four elements and four double natures, i.e. male and female, agent and patient: and he states the composition and the names of what it is, teaching that the sun is its father, and the moon its real mother, and that the wind carries it in its belly, and the earth is its nurse; it is quite clear that the wind is the air, and the air is life, and life is the soul which gives birth to and nourishes our whole work:

Dry becomes wet, wet dry
Whiteness will soon adorn black
The wise man following, by the fire which guides him,

Currently changes the white work to red.

Known and duly prepared materials that do not require otherwise come to full perfection, as you see how our water by the action of our fire reduces the quality of our material called red brass, and, hard and solid though that is, it is rendered subtle and fluid:

Latin: "The dissolution of fire comes into being in such a smooth and continuous way, until it goes forth into the water, and the whole impalpable, viscous tincture melts into the first black color." [French: And that in such a solution, the fire is soft and continuous until dissolved in water; and so firstly, all viscous impalpable excess-dye is made black, which is the sign of the true solution.]

This water is so lovely & so friendly to solar fruit that as soon as he is put in it he melts, and dissolves slowly like ice in hot water, without noise, without violence, without being destroyed, gently throwing his seed and tincturing the one he takes pleasure in and welcomes for a time; after which he comes to germinate, blossom and

be reborn with a thousand times more strength, beauty and subtlety than he had before. So here is the property of our dissolutive water, not the one of the ignorant, who wear out strong corrosive waters they call regia, herbal extractions, roots and salts that, instead of building or maintaining, destroy; in short, who do not know where to go or imagine how to find our solvent.

They will look for stinking muddy and filthy water, a hundred miles from their home. They are blind to the Source of life and clear Fountain of seven streams arising, on their doorstep and before their very eyes!

I will say no more now that makes sense to understand, but rather discover in passing what the Philosophical fire may be, without which our medicine cannot come to perfection. I was curious to browse and read the books of learned philosophers dealing with the subject of this work, and I did look for and collect the most I have been able to: such as the sermon of Hermes' commentary of

Hortulanus, Calid, Rasis, Roger Bacon, Flamel, the Rosary, Arnauld de Villeneuve, Albert the Great, Margarita Preciosa, Thesaurus Thesaurorum, Sinesius and countless others, both in rhyme and prose; and have not found in one of the aforementioned, steps marked or a passing sign that might have to do with the fire, but at last there fell into my hands a little treatise entitled Major Key of Artephius, wherein a few words were spoken:

Latin: "And our fire is mineral, equal, continuous: it does not fume unless it is stirred up too much, participates in the sulfur, and is taken from other sources than from the matter; it overturns all things, dissolves, congeals and calcines." [French: Our fire is mineral, equal and continual, and will evaporate at the point it is too excited: participating from the sulfur, and taken from outside of the material, it upsets everything, dissolves, congeals and calcines.]

So it is a mineral fire, continuously hot, vaporous and dry, altering, penetrating and digesting. Simmering, it heats the bath or fountain in which bathe the king and queen, with the aid of which the Artist leads our medicine to perfection:

One may then, in perfect silence,
Eyes still open, and away from the vanities,

Endlessly taste the fruit of the beautiful science,
Despising the residence and employment of cities.

Annotation:
This is a warning given to those who own and have reached the goal of this much desired and precious medicine, because with that, one can perform wonderful treatments by which one can greatly benefit; and recognizing such admirable effects, it is permitted to retire from the common bustle to a distant location of the world; that is to say, for more leisure to consider the wonderful and most secret effects of Nature.

Rich, one can cultivate his heritage,
Left to himself to enjoy his love,
One can get married, for his lineage to thrive,
And praise the Lord the remainder of his days.

Annotation:
Briefly, one who has this medicine and physical powder has obtained the remedy against any necessity, and what was impossible to him without it: he can make repairs without fear and inconvenience, for in a moment he can perfect what was imperfect, and heal the sick, making him healthy and fit as follows:

The miser, gouty, and paralytic
Can without fail find healing herein.
This is the liquor and physical powder
Which formerly rejuvenated good old Aeson!

Annotation:

Finally the Philosopher purposely mentions the virtue of this powder in the healing of these three peculiar accidents of life, stinginess, paralysis and gout; for even though such healing is overall or general; this feature is quoted to intimate effectiveness even with the said three diseases, which are not curable by vulgar medicine.

According to Ovid (Metamorphoses vii. 163, 250, &c.), Jason's father Aeson survived the return of the Argonauts, and was made young again by Medea.

****

Master Alchemist Khunrath: As Practiced from a Vajrayana Perspective

[For my Son Nate, who I hope may someday see the significance of these things I have written about.]

While not presuming to have the only correct interpretation of a master alchemist like Henricus Khunrath, I would like to suggest one way we can apply him, along the lines of our late esteemed friend, Sasha Shulgin's assessment of alchemy as "meditation." This approach assumes a certain universal understanding of Reality as advanced by the many perennial Wisdom traditions of both East and West. So in my case, I draw from experience of the root teachings of Indian and Tibetan Vajrayana to work with parallel resonances in Khunrath's text; taking a central passage of his core instruction as representative of how we may best apply him. Although this particular passage is from his book, Hyleal Chaos, he engages in cross-referencing here to the illustrative plates of his famous Amphitheatre of Eternal Wisdom; especially plate iii, which, from a Vajrayana perspective, is a Yidam: a divine "Self" projection that he calls the "Son of the Great World."
This is not a specifically gender-oriented figure, but rather an androgynous ideal for extracting pure Realization from the natural "chaos" of Mind with its incessant proliferation of random thought, "covering" the mind, like "mist obscuring the sun." The trick is to recognize in this raw matter, this chaotic jumble of thinking, the undiluted flow of Living Water -- Awareness!

Such a pristine cognition is non-conceptual; likened by our Author to an "Aethereal water" that arises as the sharpest, clearest "vinegar of the Wise," bathing and dissolving all entanglements of thought. The terminology is apt, because, in Vajrayana schools of practice, this perception that "cuts through" mental obscurity is "clear light" itself.

The physical basis of this water and perception is rooted in "Salt," expressive of a Universal (or as our Author says, Catholic) preservative principle; as well as the actual saline "well-spring" of the eyes. One of the primary texts of Indian and Tibetan Vajrayana schools, the Guhyasamaja-Tantra, confirms the true experience of our sense organs as "clear light": "Whatever be the sense organ and its range, each of them is light only."

This "light only" is the penetration of the discriminating filters that otherwise cloud ordinary perception. The resulting experience is, simultaneously, one of bliss and emptiness, or what is the same thing, compassion and wisdom: compassion, which is the joy of highest, all-inclusive love; wisdom which comprehends the hollow nature of seemingly separated phenomena.

Here we have the Alchemical Key that simultaneously unlocks, purifies, and regenerates things. Our Author speaks of this with a sublime eloquence that bypasses all of our superficial confusions about his imagery: "This Catholic Medicinal Well of Living Water and Oil of Gladness, now learn, thou Artful, Most Agreeable to Nature Artists, to pump and draw; so canst thy eager thirsty Art crave the very same Universal of Philosophers, flowing from this Philosophical Nectar, that in all of you gushes, refreshes, and quickens."

Referring us again to his Divine projection – the "Son of the Great World" – he admits that "Christ" is well said to be a way of signifying or symbolizing this, not in a dissimilar sense! But the Tibetan Yidam may also be considered a working model of the same. We are talking about the vivific flow of Awareness from this "Self" that simultaneously revivifies everything.

In highest Tantric systems, compassion and wisdom are typified as this secret red-and-white Nectar that flows from our purified Awareness, while the same realization is framed in the Christianized alchemical lexicon as "blood-and-water." There is both a Gnostic and an orthodox significance to the latter, in that matter as well as spirit is redeemed by this twofold, non-dual, eau de vie.

Logically following from this, Khunrath's grand conclusion is mounted upon a crescendo of the imagery we quoted from above: "A genuine Philosopher knows, believes, and confesses no other Natural Blood-and-Water that bathes, purifies, and regenerates Bodies, and can make them perfect, and more than perfect, than the dear Catholic Rosy Colored Blood-and-Aethereal Water that with Artful Power flows forth from Our Native Son of the Great World."

I only wish to add as a clarifying remark, the tremendous emphasis placed in Vajrayana on "skillful means," which is precisely our learning how to practice with the artfulness that arises from a correct understanding.

A Brief Investigation of an Initiatory Model: Swedenborg's 'Asian Society'

Spiritual locations can be accessed by travelers on different paths, just as physical or geographical ones can be approached by diverse routes through the air, on land, or by sea. Thus one metaphysical voyager who apparently happened upon an Eastern-style paradise while traveling in the "beyond" was Emanuel Swedenborg. The very origin of the inhabitants there strongly suggests this to us, as well their particular understanding and practice of what Swedenborg calls "conjugial love." And in telling us about them, Swedenborg provides some vital clues for understanding certain rituals that were later propagated in his name; although it's exceedingly doubtful that these were initiations actually conferred by him.

I am alluding here to the top two degrees of the so-called "Swedenborgian Rite" termed respectively, "Sublime" Blue Brother and "Perfect" Red Brother. But unless you give credence to unsubstantiated rumors of a "transference" of this Rite from England to Italy, where it supposedly now goes under the name of "Noah" (instead of Swedenborg); or yield to the even more dubious suggestions of certain anti-illuminati "watchdogs" that it is currently practiced in secret by the Swedenborgian theological seminary(!) my contention here will be that its only likely application in the real world today may, as a result of this study, just be you and me.

Let us begin then by decoding the two colors of "Sublime" and "Perfect" attainment in this Rite; and we will see that each "color" immediately connects to a different shade, when translated into spiritual equivalencies. The subsequent conversion of these colors is what makes for sublime and perfect understanding; which, in Swedenborgian terms, signifies perfect practice since understanding and use are symbiotically one.

This becomes clearer as we approach the initiatory model provided by Swedenborg himself in the "Second Memorable Relation" of his Conjugial Love, 76. His blissful correspondents there identify themselves as "a People in Asia" who are members of a "Silver Age" Society; and this is our first clue. When we recall that Swedenborg was appointed Extraordinary Assessor of Mines by the Swedish Crown in 1716, serving on the Board of Mines for 31 years, we may take it for granted that he was acquainted with the contemporary literature on mining and smelting techniques; which still contained many alchemical suppositions such as this one from Metallurgia: "A blue light is conceived as rising mainly from silver. So silver's tincture is blue light."

Swedenborg's Asian spirits speak to him of the "science of correspondences" as conjoining "the sensual things of our bodies with the perceptions of our minds," thus procuring for them "intelligence." And to illustrate this, they introduce him into "an ante-chamber where there were several devices on the walls, and little images as it were of molten silver." Swedenborg naturally inquires, "What are these?" He is told, "They are pictures and forms representative of several qualities, characters, and delights relating to conjugial love."

What follows is the most important part, as we learn that these walls of molten silver images reflect a rainbow, serving as a projection-screen for a sort of initiatic light-show: "While we were viewing these things, we saw as it were, a rainbow on the wall, consisting of three colors, purple (or red), blue and white; and we observed how the purple passed the blue, and tinged the white with an azure color, and that the latter color flowed back through the blue into the purple, and elevated the purple into a kind of flaming luster." The blue light arising on these silver walls provides a crucial medium for passing the purple color into the white, and returning it back to the purple in a manner that "exalts" the purple into the brilliance of flame.

What is interesting here is that blue occupies this pivotal position between the "two lights of heaven," as they are so frequently described by Swedenborg (to quote just one notable example from Divine Love and Wisdom, 380):

"In the heavens where love to the Lord reigns, the light is flame-colored, and the angels there are clothed in purple (or red) garments; and in the heavens where wisdom reigns, the light is white, and the angels there are clothed in white garments."

But here the "sublime" blue degree is intermediate to, and leading to the "perfect" red one. What is the understanding that makes this so? I would suggest the explanation provided at this point does indeed bear the stamp of a very old "Asian" tradition that may still be encountered in Shakti worship, as well as the transcendental Tantric "pure-lands" aspired to by a wide range of devotees from India, Nepal, Mongolia, and Tibet. So although it is always in terms of "the husband and wife," the explanation of conjugial love we are given, allows for a broader understanding of the "sacred pairing" that leads to divine comprehension.

As he views the walls, Swedenborg is asked, "Do you understand all this?" To which he returns the proper response of any aspiring candidate to the mysteries, "Instruct me." He is told, "The purple color signifies the conjugial love of the wife [note here that that this is already the highest color], the blue, the beginning of conjugial love in the husband's perception from the wife, and the azure, with which the white is tinged, signifies conjugial love in the husband. This latter color flowing back through the blue into the purple, and elevating the purple into a kind of flaming luster, signifies the conjugial love of the husband flowing back to the wife. Such things are represented on these walls, while from meditating on conjugial love, we view with eager attention the rainbows which are painted there!"

Samuel Beswick, the nineteenth-century renovator of the "Swedenborgian Rite," stated that he had received the craft degrees in a Swedish Lodge in England; which may just possibly link him to the London Lodges of Swedish Masonry which had enjoyed a close association with the London "Order of Heredom," whose resident engraver, Lambert de Lintot, had designed a hieroglyphical tableau quite reminiscent of the Asians' emblematic "wall." Although considerably more graphic in its depiction, than the conjoining of the "sensual things of the body" with the "perceptions of the mind" spoken of by Swedenborg's informants, the psycho-erotic implication may also be found in their presentation—borne out in no uncertain detail by the vivid sculpted walls of South Indian temples, and many another Asian location that seeks to elevate the consummation of love into a meditative act.

Swedenborg, as one who was never married, speaks to us of marriages in heaven that are, essentially, the divine conjunction in us. In tantric terms, this is called "manifesting the rainbow body," which is equivalent to the rainbow light-projections upon the wall that are viewed by Swedenborg and his hosts. We are told that the "husband" receives something already essentially divine from the light of the "wife," and must fully merge his own love into it, upon its return to her. So a prerequisite to complete the process is the assimilation of the original light of love, in the conjugial love of the "husband," which then flows back from the blue into the purple. As a very nearly similar description from the Sarva-buddhasamayayoga-tantra, announces: "Hey you who are dressed in blue, and beautified with blue ornaments, I now permit you who have received your consecration, into the circle of yoginis…." Candrakirti's tantric commentary informs us, that once they are there, they can "contemplate their conjunction with and transformation into the lady's appearance" — which for Swedenborg's "Asians" elevates her purple into a flaming luster!

I would be remiss not to say a few more words about the purple color at this point. It is, of course, the red. But in a well-documented webpage by A.J. Coriat, "The Science of Correspondences," we learn that it is specifically the ruby color — "the pure crimson of the finest rubies" — that Swedenborg means by purple. And where the "light of heaven" is flame-colored, this is the color that the angels wear.

There are immediate ramifications from this, for our understanding of the "perfect red" attainment, and for the transformation of our tantric "blue" candidate into the "lady's" appearance. The ruby color is a precise description of the transcendent yogini consort's appearance, and she is encompassed by a flaming aureole as the tantric adept communes with her. The corresponding "red" degree of the Swedenborgian Rite is likewise, an elevation of color, the marriage in heaven of the "interior man" — or at least, so far as it is genuinely derived from Swedenborg, this is the true discernment of its meaning!

At the conclusion of his interview with the Silver Age Asians, Swedenborg candidly admits on behalf of the West: "These things are more than mystical at this day," — which is not to say they should remain that way. While advanced degree "lodges" and bona fide tantric "empowerments" may appear to be especially auspicious opportunities for us, where happenstance of location and karma of circumstance permit this, we already possess the most important thing spoken of in this short essay: awareness that there is a higher lover. This awareness may not be perfect, but it approaches the "sublime" when we begin to experience our love as the "return" of a prior love, repaid with interest.

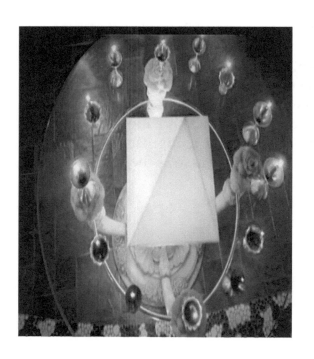

THE SPRING EQUINOX SELF-ENACTED ELUS COHEN RITE OF RECONCILIATION & ADOPTION

Compiled from Original Documentation
By Russell Yoder

✸✸✸✸✸✸✸✸✸✸✸✸✸✸✸✸✸✸✸✸✸✸✸✸✸✸

The Elus Cohen tradition of Martinez de Pasqually provides us with at least one essential process for receiving a personal manifestation of reconciliation or 'divine adoption' — intentionally timed to coincide with the first five days of the Spring Equinox. While of course there is no guarantee of precisely what an aspirant may or may not experience by actually doing this, a few simple steps ensure the correct preparation of the chamber of operation, as well as the proper comportment of oneself. Specific formularies of prayer or petition are mostly omitted here: these can be inserted from Martinist, Masonic, or far more personal resources of one's own.

The exact times, dates, sequence and duration of the personal ritual undertaken commence with the preparation of the chamber of operation, at the hour of the Equinox itself. This requires the tracing of a quarter circle, wedge or angle, the point of whose apex is at the center of the Eastern side of the chamber. A circle is drawn inside of this, with three candles or luminaries in a row, North to South. Additional luminaries may be placed outside the circle in the three points of the angle. On the central candle, or within the circle itself, inscribe the hieroglyph RAP, for the Mediator or Protector, Raphael* — one of two especially invoked to convey one's request for a clear token of spiritual adoption.

*"One who heals in the name of the Lord": the 'Angel' named in the Book of Tobias, who teaches the hero there about reciting the requisite magical recipes, as well as preparing the fumigations and unctions which put to flight 'demons'; invoked by the Elus Cohens as a particularly powerful defender.

The other Mediator, IAB in the original document (although some prefer IAH or IAO), may be considered the Coadjutant of your Higher Power — whose own circle is placed just inside the entrance to your chamber. One large consecrated candle is placed in the center of the latter circle, where you again inscribe the three-letter hieroglyph of this Mediator.

The two straight lines radiating out from the Eastern point of the quarter circle must be slanted at an angle wide enough to enclose a hexagon around a circle that can comfortably contain the kneeling and prostrating figure of yourself as the Operant. The hexagon is considered the 'Talismanic Shield' whose points are directed against the presence of any inimical influences; and may be consecrated by you, with the letters R,A,P individually placed in the three Eastern-most points, North to South; and I,A,B likewise filling the three points to the West.

Allowing enough time to accomplish the preliminaries, before you actually kneel within your own circle of petition at precisely 10:00 in the evening on the Day of the Equinox; enter the chamber and light the single candle within the circle of IAB, saying: "Blessed is He Who assists me and understands me, O Bagniakim, Amen."*

*Insofar as the appeal here is to the Coadjutant of your Higher Power, there is a Traditional implication that the Revelator of these Rites, Pasqually, comprises a portion of this Spiritual Advocate.

Proceed to the circle within the Eastern angle and kindle each of the six luminaries inside and around it, starting with the centermost candle of the circle. Finally, kneel within your own circle, and prostrate with your forehead pressed to the carpet or floor, facing East.

You should be clothed in comfortably clean white cotton or linen clothes, specially reserved for this occasion; although not a dress or a robe, as you will need a clear view through the aperture of your legs, for the latter part of each evening's meditation. (I should add an important word of confirmation here from my study of both the Scottish Gaelic and indigenous Thai magical traditions: namely, that the spiritual manifestation sought is to be perceived precisely as described in what follows: Rev. Robert Kirk's The Secret Commonwealth may be consulted for a sample specimen of this from the former culture.)

Your meditation in this position is undertaken for precisely one half-hour, on each of five successive evenings, commencing with the Day of the Spring Equinox itself. You will however time this event so as to begin half an hour later each evening; thus following the sequence of 10:00, 10:30, 11:00, 11:30, and culminating with 12:00 midnight over the course of five days.

This creates a certain crescendo of its own, and the potency increases with each session thus observed. However, it should be clarified that reception of a clear sign by you, on any of the five evenings, allows you to conclude the Operation at that time, with proper acknowledgment of thanks. (Such is of course a matter of truly genuine discernment on your part.)

Additional preparations by you may include (although not specifically mandated), fasting and a ritual bath, and allowance of a light repast by you, following each night's session; and in general, a much condensed version of the mindful vigil undertaken by the "Faithful" during the week of the Quranic "Night of Power" which concludes Ramadan.

One devotes slightly better than one half of each night's session to the inward call; in the position of prostration (that is, with forehead touching the floor, and hands placed slightly forward on either side of the head). The proper attitude of the aspirant —and the most sound approach to adopt — is best summed up in this poignant appraisal of the entire business undertaken in ritual work by the Elus Cohens:

"Their Theurgia, respectful of the unlimited power of dignity, does not more than address their Emissaries, and is not intended to force them to appear other than with the consent of the Infinite Power upon Whom they are dependent; and as proof of the graces that the future life reserves for the elect."

One is bowing then to that unseen Author of Blessing; and, through petition and prayer, extending one's humble, honest hope that the Mediators permitted to past Elus Cohens for this purpose, may also encourage you with a similar conciliatory token of grace, as it is given them to deliver:

"That is, during the Operation, in the domain bounded by the circles and quarter circle where they 'appear' the major Spirits, carriers of Good Intellect, Energy, and Divine Intelligence, may, if permitted, be sent to announce that one is 'adopted' or in other words, reconciled with the Divine."

The rest of the procedure follows fairly directly from this. During the time remaining in each evening's session, the aspirant, with open eyes, turns the attention to the circle designated by the hieroglyph IAB, "precisely watching only the shining luminary of this hieroglyph, between the legs."

(Note that one remains in the same position throughout the half-hour dedicated to this purpose each evening.) With a relaxed one-pointed focus, one concentrates upon the flame and immediate proximity of the circle it illuminates (simply that). Any clear anomalies of whatever nature that are perceived during this time are to be accepted as your sign; so be sure that you are paying sufficient attention to what is happening!

Do not extend your vigil beyond the half-hour appointed for these five evenings of the Rite. Also refrain from increasing the number of sessions beyond the final one at midnight. These parameters are established for intentional esoteric reasons. (If you feel a strong need to pursue further confirmation, wait until next year at the same time.)

After finishing your prostration, with its concluding observation of the hieroglyphic luminary just inside the entrance of your chamber; arise and extinguish the lights of the quarter circle, in reverse order to the way you enkindled them; and do likewise with the single candle you had been contemplating, before withdrawing from the chamber of operation.

A number of additional suggestions may be made at this point:

As with many Magical procedures, it is helpful to maintain a journal of the entire experience, whether or not it is punctuated with something of a 'dramatic' nature. The insights arising, even from your deliberately cultivating this posture of receptivity and expectant waiting, can lead you to a deeper level of understanding that in turn may sensitize you to spiritual phenomena in general.

For those who have expressed concern to me about having sufficient space in their apartments or homes for the ritual layout, as described here; it is most important to just have a room that is set aside exclusively for this purpose, during the week of enacting the Rite. You may asperge or purify it and its contents, utilizing any traditional method for this purpose.

The Mediators' two circles may be 'miniaturized' a bit by employing two round stands or low-lying small tables for placing the candles or luminaries on. Only the three within the circle of RAP and the single light within that of IAB are requisite. The important thing is to maintain a clear line of sight to the latter while prostrating.

The only circle that must be 'full-size' is your own, sufficient to accommodate you without cramping. The encompassing hexagon may, however, be dispensed with and replaced with a Seal of Solomon-type hexagram worn around the neck, to serve as your Talismanic Shield.

With regards to the petition, prayer, or invocation you use, personal ownership of the process is extremely important here. Stilted formularies which bear little resemblance to your own innermost convictions will hardly 'actualize' into something of significance! (Those who disagree with this position are of course welcome to resort to older formulas.)

One 'non-negotiable' aspect, however, is the choice of Mediators or Protectors that are specified in this Rite. They are as inherent to this process as 'Olympian Spirits' and 'Dharma Protectors' are to similar operations or empowerments of an Eastern or Western nature. They constitute the Seal of the Elus Cohen approach to the Mysteries; and are sufficiently 'inclusive' to allow most practitioners of the monotheistic traditions to honor this approach without discomfort.

At least implicit in all of the foregoing is the understanding that however the specific 'manifestation' is perceived by you, it should have an impact, either immediate or of a more gently-unfolding nature, within you. Here again, your journal may be of invaluable assistance in recording the ongoing nuances of this! The overriding idea is of a new beginning — indeed a 'freeing up' of a divinely-intended latency within you — that at last has found its egress into the mundanities of life, and made of them a world of new possibilities for you.

****

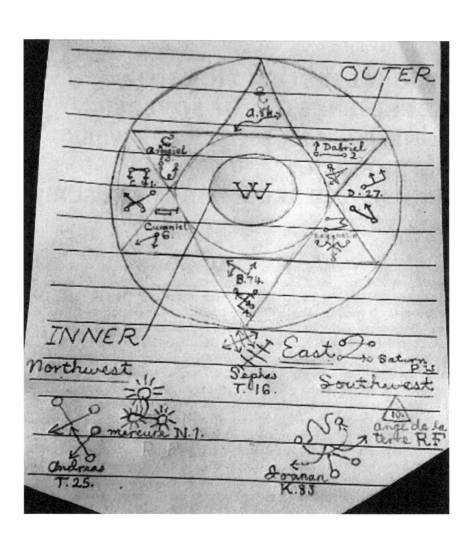

PERSONAL INSTRUCTION WORK, IN THE PRESENCE OF THE SOVEREIGN ALONE: FOR ANY DAY OF THE WEEK WHATSOEVER.
(TRANSLATED FROM THE "MANUSCRIT D'ALGER")

"The operant will especially and strongly address his patrons and his guardian, in order to know who they are. If the operant often has the same character before his eyes either by day or by night, it is probable that it is that of his guardian; he will therefore place it next to the latter's real name, and will also ask him for confirmation, either in this same work, or in a dream or vision. The operant may specifically request the repetition and confirmation of such characters, names, and letters that have affected him most at the time. I would advise an operant to be alone in his operation, and this to avoid the confusion and the uncertainty of knowing for whom the passes and appearances are intended. This work can be done indifferently any day of the week, one day only, or three days in a row; I suggest the latter course instead, because one can obtain on the second or the third day what one would not have obtained in a single day, and, moreover, the operant is better disposed the second and third day than on the first. One must have the attention of the Spirit of the planet of the day, whenever one calls his patrons or his guardian. It is best to avoid the confusion of making too large a quantity of requests at the time: faith, hope, charity, amen."

THESE STRAIGHTFORWARD AND SENSIBLE DIRECTIONS FROM THE "MANUSCRIT D'ALGER" ARE AMONG MY VERY FAVORITES! IT IS CLEARLY A "PERSONAL WORKING" TO BE UNDERTAKEN CONFIDENTIALLY IN ONE'S OWN SANCTIFIED SPACE, WITH ONLY THE SOVEREIGN AS "WATCHER"; PRIOR TO WHATEVER PETITION OR ADDRESS YOU MAKE FOR AWARENESS OF YOUR INDIVIDUAL MENTORS.

I WOULD SUGGEST IT IS MOST *ESSENTIAL* TO DETERMINE THE IDENTITY OF YOUR PERSONAL "GUARDIAN" FIRST, AND THEN AFTERWARDS, YOU CAN ASK FOR A MENTAL OR PHYSICAL CONFIRMATION OF ANY ADDITIONAL "CHARACTERS, NAMES, AND LETTERS" TO ASSIST IN IDENTIFYING *OTHER* "PATRONS".

BECAUSE OF MY BACKGROUND IN THE "EPHRATA TRADITION" I ONLY ENGAGE THIS OPERATION ON *SATURDAYS;* AND INSTEAD OF TWO OR THREE DAYS IN A ROW, I REPEAT IT ON *SUCCESSIVE SABBATHS* AS NEEDED. ALSO, A MOST POTENT DAILY "CALL" FROM "MANUSCRIT D'ALGER" HAS BEEN REVEALED TO ME, AS *PREFATORY* ADDRESS FOR THE SPIRITS OF THAT DAY (WHO ARE, APPROPRIATELY, *BOTH SOLAR AND SATURNIAN*).

YOU WILL NOTICE IN THE PARTIAL WORKING "TABLEAU" OR FREEHAND *SKETCH* OF MINE THAT I'VE ATTACHED, A *VERTICAL* ARRANGEMENT OF: "CHARACTER, HIEROGLYPH, AND NAME" ON THE APPROPRIATE "LOCATIONS" WHEN ALL THREE OF THESE DATUMS ARE PROVIDED.

UNIQUE TO THE TRADITION WE HAVE RECEIVED FROM MARTINES DE PASQUALLY IS AN ENTIRELY *NEW* THEO-MAGICAL RECONFIGURING OF OTHERWISE FAMILIAR "ANGELIC, APOSTOLIC, AND PROPHETIC" NAMES (AND EVEN THEIR *PROPER SPELLINGS*): THESE ARE DERIVED FROM A PECULIAR LETTER-NUMBER *ALGEBRA,* THAT IS DISTINCTLY PASQUALLY'S OWN; AND *SHOULD NOT* BE CONFUSED WITH OTHER SOURCES, SUCH AS JEWISH KABBALAH, MEDIEVAL GRIMOIRE, OR CATHOLIC CATECHISM.

"ATTRIBUTIONS" MAY ALSO APPEAR *DIFFERENT,* SUCH AS THE VERY SIGNIFICANT ELUS-COHEN UNDERSTANDING OF "RAPHAEL" AS THE *ANGEL OF THE EARTH:* AND WHERE "PLANETARY" DESIGNATIONS ARE INDICATED, SUCH AS MERCURY AND SATURN, UNDERSTAND THE "ANGELS" THEREOF, NAMELY NURIEL AND PHANUEL – *ALL OF WHOM* ARE INTENDED AS SPECIAL WARDS FOR ORIENTING US *WITHIN* THE MAGICAL SPACE OF A GIVEN OPERATION (THUS, *CHANGING* FROM ONE WORKING TO ANOTHER, ACCORDINGLY).

IF WE MANAGE TO *ACCEPT* THIS IDIOSYNCRATIC METHOD OF WORKING *WITHIN* SPECIFIC LITTLE WORLDS FOR THE ACCOMPLISHMENT OF BENEFICIAL PURPOSES, IT CAN *RECONFIGURE US;* ENABLING RELEVANT, AND SOMETIMES ASTONISHING, CHANGES IN OUR *OWN* SEEMINGLY-FIXED PARAMETERS; AS NOTED HERE IN A COMPARATIVE SENSE BY GEORGES COURTS:

"In the works of Castaneda, Don Juan Matus demonstrates that time and space are only a personal vision and that this vision can totally change. By sacralizing space, and by incorporating personal and universal energies, the emulator creates a kind of magical universe, where time can accelerate or slow down, and space can be condensed and transformed. The Indians say that we then excite a center or chakra called "Bindou", where time and space seem to be confused, with the perception of powers beyond ordinary vision. For example, knowing the past and the future would become possible, just as visiting other worlds, with the image of becoming infinitely large or infinitely small. For Martinès, it is the *good* spirits who will be called, and who will give this knowledge, by evocation or invocation."

I WOULD ALSO LIKE TO CONCLUDE THIS BRIEF STUDY WITH A FAVORITE QUOTATION OF MINE, AS TRANSLATED BY ME FROM ONE OF PASQUALLY'S VERY LAST LETTERS:

"For it will only be by yourself and by your own understanding that you will manage to instruct and train yourself, either in work or in interpretation. You should not be alarmed however; instead **redouble** your courage and confidence in the certainty that your time and happiness will not fail to happen if you want it, for indeed man is their master."

"HEDGE WIZARD": SELECTED VERSES OF RUSSELL YODER

"DOWN TO INVERNESS" – A teardrop in a mother's eye / sends ripples through the sky. / Down some sweet corridor of unknown grace / there waits for each his special place, / obscure to most and higher / than where outward stars inwardly spin. / It only takes a moment's pause / for us to say, "Away, away, / our purposes are far afield! / We played the game merely to win, / and found instead a specter's grin." / The cock has crowed, the moonlight host / of Fairy Folk and Holy Ghost / have left the field, the fools thereon, / like land-locked salmon / who thought to spawn; / and as our eyes become blank scales / on midden heaps and coal-black shales, / one question lingers like the womb. / Should we begin to love our tomb? / Like revenants we crave the marrow / of recent life and fallen sparrow. / Yet solace is the chain of lakes / that trickles down to Inverness. / White heron land, lotus abode / indigo waters cobalt cold. / Call it peace or call it death, / journey now and let love rest.

"HIDDEN IMAM" - On humble donkey / all the way to Sijistan, / Beneath the moon / rode forth the Sun. / Clad in coarse black / Sufi shawl, / Self-annihilated / the One of All.

"GROVES" - I walk in groves Osiris green, / the gold of life there plainly seen. / The emerald Lion proclaims his vow, / heaven in earth is here and now. / The stars are nature's holy wells, / the breath of life contains their spells. / Seven phases define the moon, / a Rose of light that rises soon.

"ROSICRUCIAN" —
The man of rose satin.
Five apertures: eyes as triple orbs,
govern his breathing, speaking.
Attended by a universal Luna,
such Earth is smoothed all over
with Balsam, flowing cruciform
from this Light-station.

"AL-KHEM" - Mother Binah's unseen net / holds the Theatre of the Universe. / A tenebrous stage appears thereon, / Delta chaos of blackest Khem. / In sheerest linen, maid fills her jar / at the lapping edge of Inundation. / Contents that glimmer leaven within: / "Take ye the thyrsus, drink of the cup." / Osiris rises, jeweled like a lion. / The Eleusinian secret is within thee! / Salt of wonder, productive of wine, / Corn newly green on Dionysus' wand.

"ARROYO" - Mesquite dripping branches / in frond fringed arcs, / straw colored reeds / straight up to the sky, / lizards that scurry / fast as the rabbits, / coffee with milk / pretending to flow. / Lagoons of old Venice / but really south Texas, / where soul flies erratic / beside the calm ducks, / breezes just tease here / but gnats own the moment, / pause and absorb this / dilution of madness.

"OASIS" - A circle of desert, where salt sand and sky, choose greenery to greet thee, like tapers rising high, O Isis Osiris, secret fire from afar.

"VIRGINIA STORM" - Tiny glow flies named for lightning / streak the green sward through my window, / while pink arcs of the real stuff / carve sigils with a magic sword, / in the twilight draped behind the tree line. / Then the rain comes and blurs it all, / with a steady thrum that washes even the thunder.

"MAJESTIC GLANCE" (Dedicated to 2 Magi: Jacob Boehme & Conrad Beissel) - What if a roseate / beam returned / from the West, / kindling sweet liquorous / vapours of air; / And riding the surge of / the sudden / coral Sea, / angelic song birds laid / a carpet to dance?

"STELLAR VINTAGES" - They are dusky casks / in a wine cellar, / infinite sizes / from which you can tap, / along with the dust / of stars in your dust, / vintage stuff well-steeped! / Lighter kinds abound; / but for "iron" choose / the potent dwarf grapes / which draw off the sap / from their bright sisters. / And if truth be told, / far stranger than tales, / fellow traveler / "gold" is the harvest / of storms quite foreign / to here! The dark rains / come down, with pollen / unseen, and sow in / our orchard a rich / nitrum green.

"SNOW FIELD" - Is it possible / the gulfs of space / are matched by / the infinity / of a snow field? / Diamond constellations / overwhelming / in number: / golden Sols strewn, / archangel reds, / eye piercing blues, / solder-hot whites; / and lastly, / the distraction / of demon seed, / variable Algols, / baffling the sight / that thirsts for Clear Light.

FROM THE "COOL-PSALMS" OF QUIRINIUS KUHLMANN (translated by Russell Yoder) - Formed directly from Your Tree, / at present only twigs; / all of them wanting, desiring, / this one, that one! / Yet all of them far-spreading poison at the end. / There Boehme* desists, / as he bears witness to me, / one of scarcely ten / in a reckoning of millions. / There nothing that is full / of Self-will passes away. / So it is impossible for me / to be with such people! / Wanton pride signifies / what they choose to draw / from the eternal Wonder wheel of Seven.
*See dedication to "Majestic Glance."

"SECRET SONG" - There's a jukebox / in the corner / rattling out / its tinny tune, / lost in the machinery / woven on a strange loom. / If the Artist / can unloose it / then he has / the whole world, / a singular Pearl / popping out / of its shell.

"CINNABAR WANDERER" –
I live in a Green Place, with Whom You have given me,
And You remind me of Calls received,
Wherever You have Placed me: high winding trails,
Windswept and open, hovering above Caramelized canyons
Of Yellow-ochre, melting red rock;
Serenely set for our Encounter,
As You have again recalled for me Today!
Grandmother, *Your Cooking is so Sweet*....

"WRITTEN TRANSMISSION" –

Oft times I'd like to milk the Sun/ and squeeze its homogeneous/ Nectar into the lives of All/ who've ascended the Noosphere:/ so that We could scribe the Northern/ Lights in visible ink of a/ fluid Electricity,/ cross-referencing and collating/ thus, our Sacred Writ of Infinity!

"ALCHEMICAL MASQUE" –
Your lineage is rooted in the Tree. Heart-wise philosophers watch over Thee. / To honor them, fair Maidens dance; Masked Mercury is there, and not by chance! / Chains of Love are all that bind, but Earth is never left behind. / Your clearing is a Magic zone, with tools of Art you carefully hone. / Peacock, raven, serpent, and skull; discrimination thus annul. / Spacious Wonder that you unfold is crystal-bright compared to Gold. / Soul arises when Mind is clear, behold Your Nature in the Mirror.

"EQUIPOISE" -
In a cliff-house,
merely a higher octave of this plain earth,
I embrace you;
though the air is displaced
by the immensity of
a passing star voyager,
we rejoice in the language of the birds.

"EVENING STAR" - Le voyageur, blood of Merovee (and Phoenician before), graced his Huron upon both cheeks; conjunct in their slender alembic of bark, poised on incandescent liquid sheet, threading their pearl to where now lay, westward on lowering violet bed—Astarte!
"ASCENDING OFF THE GRID" - Mother, I have been a dancing Sow, weaving what I sew./ In Conyers, drank the roses up a slope,/ yielding to your leaven, Binah, all the way to heaven./ Every thought, an Empty fullness now, gone aloft — home-bound:/ Departing present port for the Pyramidal town./ We calcinate at dawn—then Rubify, evoking every bone's Colossal sigh.

"The Downfallen Two Who Cured Elvishly!" (A True Account)
Lone warbler in the dusk, / Trilling her inquiry / that turned a Twilight key / in the fair downy Hill / of Isabel Halfdane / and Scotch lass Jonet Troll: / Now hardly Keltic girls! / these Viking-descended / sisters from bonny Perth / Town, / sentenced for doing / healings, by Presbyters / quite proper in their plaids. / Faeries or no, behind / this blasted business: / simply not Authorized!

****

AXIS MUNDI WITHIN THE OUROBOROS OCEAN" (A CREATIVE ADAPTATION OF PGM IV)

Adapted from the Papyri Grecae Magicae IV, lines 2715 to 2784:

The Magician stands erect, as cosmic Mountain, within an envisioned Ouroboros circle of all-encompassing Okeanos (the ever-flowing Stream of Seven Waters).
He proclaims the voces magicae: AKRODÊRE! ("Eater of the tip of your tail" — referring to the **Ouroboros**, used here as the secret name for invoking **Hekate**, Mediator to the primordial and ancestral "serpent" power)
COME, Hekate, Virgin having Many Names: Koura, Goddess, Guard and Shield, Persephona, Three-Headed, Intimate of Fire, Cow-Eyed, All-Consuming!

This simultaneous **Calling to the Deep** — the subterranean base of one's own axis mundi, **Source** of Hekate's hidden Shakti-springs —enables the **Sun** to rise from **Okeanos** in the East: This Deep is also the **Womb of Isis**, connected to the **Nile River**. And **Osiris** (the ancient Egyptian identity of **Orion**) was first of all a man, showing us the way to transform our own mortal nature into an immortal soul, filled with the **Light** that is the Breath of God flowing from the Womb of the Goddess.
Pronounce the voces magicae: MOUISRÔ! ("Lotus, Lion, Ram": phonetic reference to **Ra-Khepri-Atum** — the **Sun's meridian path**, east-zenith-west or morning-midday-evening)
Envision the Sun reaching its *zenith* above the cosmic Mountain and your crown.

Pronounce the voces magicae:
CHARCHAR (KAHAR-KAHAR) ADÔNAI ZEUS! (Respectful titles to signify "lords") **YOU, Orion and Michael, enthroned above, now hold Power over the Seven Waters and the Earth, as Summoner of the great Serpent.**
Extending upwards to its full length along the Magician's spine as cosmic Mountain, the great Serpent "ignites" his magical Mind.

Pronounce the final voces magicae:
DÊ DAMNAMENEUS KYNOBIOU EZAGRA! (Secret reference to the **oracular Serpent spirit** of the "hero cult" — an empowered way of peaceful **departing**, to offer one's light to the ancestral or "mighty dead")

With the accomplishment of the "Crowning" the great Serpent sinks back down along the spine, as the Sun descending into the west of Okeanos (behind you). In this way, your illuminated Awareness comes to rest in the place of the *ancestral heroes.*

Buried in the Breast (a Tale of Northwest Passage) Alternative Reality Fiction

At the beginning of the New Ice Age, Raphael found his holy Grail tucked in the shade of North Mountain, near the junction of the settled lands and the beckoning sprawl of Virginia's Northwestern Territories. His father Paul hearkened to the siren song of the "Virgin's" undiscovered parts, with a lust that belied his age; having already brought the entire family to perch in readiness on the ledge of civilization's borders. But while he prepared his offspring to leap into what lay beyond, one peculiar and sedentary son uncovered a relic of mystery closer to hand. Raphael the son concealed his excitement behind a suggestion that his father Paul go forward into the Northwest to scout out choice pickings. Banking on the fire of enthusiasm that was already there, he was able distract an old man who was all too often leery of his son's inexplicable hesitations. But Raphael knew he must prepare the ground carefully for his father's acceptance, and for that he needed time.

Until recently, Paul would have been delighted at any show of enthusiasm on Raphael's part for his immediate surroundings. Which was just a way of admitting that Raphael was not looking for what he found, where he found it. Hitherto, the most unusual bit of local lore he had unearthed was a story of some people holed up on a farm in the last century looking for the Second Coming. But that was a far cry from the solid artifact of the Ephraim Society that stood, unremarked upon by history, on a stretch of fallow land below the mountain.

A high box of finely-lathed overlapping planks grew up into a Gothic crown interspersed with a series of very narrow dormers. While a superficial glance might have mistaken such Old-World eccentricity for an elegant though weathered upcountry Virginia barn, Raphael thrilled with immediate recognition at the sight of this unreported haven of the secret "diaspora".

All of his life, from the epiphanic moment when he first stood before the hallowed, now empty buildings of Constantin Bessel's original Ephraim settlement on the green tidal plain of Virginia, he had yearned to follow the trail of its pilgrim seed-bearers on their mission of esoteric planting in the New World. He knew it was the only possible way to trace the fate of those who had gone west, carrying the "Grain Buried in the Breast" of their mystical Founder.

While John Chapman ("Appleseed") followed a parallel mission to the North, planting orchards in his wake, the Bessel "brothers" were rumored to erect telltale log replicas of the Founder's occult monastery downstate. These relics were considered to be a witness to their passing residence of a season or two in such places, before moving on to new horizons. In a supremely ironic manner, Raphael's obsession with finding such artifacts paralleled Paul's own restless lunge away from civilization towards the beckoning Northwest.

But no one, including Johnny the Apple-lover, had anticipated the sudden shift of the Ice southward into Man's domain. The Northern states had already emptied out or been squeezed into narrow coastal corridors. And even locally, North Mountain bore Glacial creepings along its leeward side, close to the appropriately named "World's End" waterfalls and swimming hole, which had been Raphael's only previous love in this land of frontier desolation to which his father had brought the family.

Now the only hope for a Northwest Passage out of "Canaan's" limitations lay in those unbordered tracts of Virginia dominion extending endlessly towards a polar Occident without end. Or at least that's what the original Colony Charter had said. There was a great River to the West, and even Greater Lakes beyond. But to listen to Paul, that was just the start. Somehow the globe's truncation resulting from the abrupt polar shift had created a clear corridor with favorable climatic conditions to be found nowhere else on Earth. Caught up in his own private fantasy, Raphael remained more than a little dubious of his father's unshaken conviction.

But it was necessary to humor the old man sufficiently to get him out of the way. Raphael could be remarkably calloused and selfish when it came to realizing his own dreams. And in this, there was more than a passing similarity between father and son. It was a happily foregone conclusion then, when Paul set out on his odyssey, along with his doting and dour wife (Raphael's stepmother), and Raphael's two younger brothers. All that was required of the eldest son was his promise to follow, as soon as his peculiar "research" was finished. Paul's tolerance of even this was tempered only by the knowledge that his prodigal offspring had found a reason to "like" the place Paul had originally transplanted the family to -- a confirmation of the father's own excellent judgment!

Nothing of the Constantin Bessel fascination entered into Raphael's family conversations. Matters of the Spirit had always been prosaic and dutiful for his kinfolk. Indeed, any reference to the heretical colonial patriarch had been suppressed in table-talk of the family, during the years of growing up at home, even though the empty lodgings of the Founder's cloister lay so near at hand.

Raphael always felt he had been deliberately deprived of his "real" birthright, after the almost accidental visit to Ephraim that resulted in his earth-shaking epiphany. But even then he was careful to minimize the nature of his "conversion" experience, lest Paul attempt to root out yet again the inborn folly of his most impractical son. It was alright to be a visionary as long as that vision extended solely to the pioneer conquest of matter! And so all that Paul really knew about his son's latest obsession was that it involved renovating a historical "property" he had found beside North Mountain. Paul was actually slightly amused that he had never noticed the property himself! But by then he was so gung-ho to start on his new trek, that he could not take the time to assess the true value of what his son had stumbled upon.

That, of course, was Raphael's stratagem, and a carefully orchestrated part of his dissembling. With father and brothers safely removed, he concluded a hasty purchase of the weed-choked lot containing the derelict building, and set to work on the interior, privately forestalling disclosure of the secret identity of the property. The season was well advanced, and already a black hoarfrost clung to virtually everything in the path of the sluggish grey, glacial behemoth overtaking North Mountain. Raphael's labors were extensive, and Paul would have been amazed at how practical his son's skills actually were. Part of the perversity of the generational disconnect between them was Raphael's hiding of his manual dexterity!

Yet the interior rot was so fargone that Raphael felt a panic welling up inside him, threatening to topple him irrevocably into the darkness of the season. Only one thing saved him in the midst of this twilight crisis. On a whitewashed upstairs wall, cracked plaster over lathed boards, was a faded stencil even more significant than his original discovery of the building. It bore a mandala-like design of a figure holding an open book in one hand and a circle of stars in the other, with a sprout or branch extending from the right side of his breast and a rose over his heart. Instantly Raphael was consumed by a holocaust capable of melting every glacier in sight! Without the shadow of a doubt, a planting of the "Grain Buried in the Breast" was bestowed on him. Henceforward, no one could foreswear him, not even Paul! He possessed the proof that the secret Mission had passed this way.

Over the months that followed, he fashioned for himself a little cell in that upstairs chamber, tinted pink by the East-West bleeding of a weakened sun, but radiating a glow of certainty for him that all would be well, as long as he centered himself here for the rest of his life.

Such of course was not left unchallenged. After forestalling the inevitable hand-carried summons of his father, borne to his door by travelers returning from the "Territories"; he received a visit from his younger brother Seth in the Spring. A sibling who possessed all the pugnacity of the elder version, his brother presented him with a simple ultimatum: either prove the extent of his renovations in a way that demonstrated his inability to leave, or lock down the place long enough to pay a visit to the family and deliver his pitch there! In the end Raphael had to concede. Truth was that he had he done very little outside the "secret chamber" since his discovery of it. The ramshackle state of everything else would only prove the lie of what he said!

Thus he only succeeded in keeping Seth at arm's length while he secured the house with bolts and chains. Together they set out through the gap beyond North Mountain that was supposedly the last remaining egress from "Canaan's" doomed shores; although Raphael doubted the truth of this severely, in light of his own private "revelations". Also, for a last chance at exodus, there were surprisingly few hardy souls upon the trail with them!

Nevertheless, what lay beyond amazed him, and rightly so. The glinting palisade of glacier blue blended at a distance with skies forming the athwart angle of their forward progress. The frozen sheet of several Great Lakes denoting the last known verge of Northwest Virginia whizzed by the two horsemen, as if the Earth had indeed folded in upon itself. And finally there was the momentous land bridge over a Strait, reflected merely by a dull, withdrawn and pacified sea rather than a roaring surf.

A hobbled horse broke the rhythm of their rapid progress; and with bones scarcely less aching than those of his distressed mount, Raphael took the occasion to steal a loft apart from his brother in the crude wayside inn they found beyond the Strait. The evanescent glimpses he espied during preceding nights now unfolded like a celestial lotus in the heavens before him. An auroral ring of palest pink, distinctly circular in shape, shimmered steadily in place over the compass Pole. He thought of the elegantly mute figure on his wall, with the seed-grain and the rose upon its breast, as he gazed at this mysterious pronouncement of the sky. But his reverie was broken by the soft shishing of fabric behind him.

Glancing back he saw that the innkeeper's daughter was holding out to him a sturdy crock of steaming porridge. Thanking her, he gestured to the mounded straw beside him and asked her to sit. She gathered up her muslin skirts and perched as tentatively as a bird. "What do you think it means?" he swept his hand in the direction of the boreal display. Her immediate response was a laugh. "I think it means we're smart to have come here, and to just let the ice have what we left in our past." The bluntness of her answer surprised him. "Maybe there are still some things worth salvaging back there," he replied. "I'm sorry, but I think not!" She again took him by surprise with her forthright manner; so much so that he found himself unable to answer. After a moment's pause, she continued. "I mean it's almost like a rehearsal for death. We have to leave everything then too, so why not get used to it." Raphael studied her like a distant landscape; brown hair the color of autumn leaves framed a delicate high cheek line, with eyes of a strange violet shade perfectly complimenting the subdued mauve stuff of her dress. Finally he asked in almost a whisper: "What is your name?" "I am Sophie, sir, and I hope I have not upset you. I suppose that's why it's good I am out here, away from the need for too many manners." "Not at all, your outlook is refreshing," he managed. "I'm just unable to share it." She seemed as drawn to his mystery as he was to hers, and they conversed long past the point his soup had cooled. Sophie offered to reheat it for him, but he declined, in favor of their continuing acquaintance. The warmth of her so near at hand stirred in him an elegant candor to which she offered encouragement, saying, "Perhaps the people of your secret society are here. That may be the only part of their secret you haven't found yet." Much as he was drawn to her, he found himself resisting the notion, as though it had come from Paul or even Seth, rather than from her. Fortunately the moment was lost in a budding affection which required no agreement.

Not sure how much of what transpired that night was fact rather than fantasy, Raphael took uncertain leave of the place the following morning with Seth. More and more the ambiguity of their destination haunted him. "Have we crossed into Canada, or is this Russia?" he wondered aloud as they progressed across silvery steppes of undulating grass. "Almost there," was all Seth would volunteer, "and don't be suggesting to anyone that the Charter of Virginia doesn't apply here!" As the day advanced, their mounts succumbed to a contagion of excitement that required stern handling. Even as they approached a tree-lined knoll within the ocean of rhythmically bending stalks, Raphael spotted the reason why; herds of grazing bison, and shaggy great elephants of some kind, like substantial cloud shadows upon the land.
"Welcome to a kinder future than you figured on having!" Paul bear-hugged him at the entrance to the cabin he and the boys had erected near the edge of the forested elevation. "A view of the good earth, and game to fill the belly all around! And what's more, my son, no ice will come here. Ask Nature herself," he swept his hand in an all-encompassing arc. "Now you are staying, of course." (Of course! He had not even had a chance to properly digest the view.) "Dad, it's great. It's all great," he responded lamely. "I found some amazing history that I believe continues somewhere out here." "Well that's just perfect! See what happens when you stick with your old man?" Further elaboration was impossible at the moment, which was probably for the better. But late that night, unable to sleep despite sheer exhaustion, Raphael envisioned his mystic wall-stencil beaming from its breast the rays of pink aurora to thaw the ice and swell the Falls at World's End into a mighty cataract.

"I can only concede that my sons should go back for one reason," Paul announced the following evening, after they had all feasted upon buffalo steaks. "I cannot provide you with wives out here! But certainly there must be a great many young women dying to leave there, before it's too late." Raphael bit down an observation that they had noticed no great exodus of Virginians on the trail, clamoring for escape. Eli, the youngest, as always nodded in agreement with their father. But Seth surprised Raphael, saying, "There are women enough if you know where to look here. Take that capable filly at the inn past the Lakes. I warrant you there aren't many finer-looking than her downstate!" Paul was already clapping Seth on the back in a congratulatory manner, but Raphael, consumed with sudden jealousy, wondered just how well Seth really knew her. His thoughts were again interrupted as Seth abruptly turned to him. "Raphael already purchased that property he said he was writing a history about! I didn't get a good look, because he was so anxious to see you, Pa!" He winked in a conspiratory manner at Raphael as the others guffawed loudly. But Paul quickly resumed a sober and businesslike mien, turning his full attention upon Raphael. "That is money thrown to the wind, son! And even though we have not much use for the stuff out here, it still doesn't grow on trees. There may come a time soon enough when the pecuniary institutes of Virginia situate themselves close by us, where they have a chance at a future, and, of course, to collect interest—the rascals!"

Raphael had not yet resolved how to broach the subject of his acquisition; but as usual, the initiative had been stolen from him. So he decided to make a clean breast of it, in the face of odds that were predictably the same. All he could really do at this point was to cover his retreat.

"There were other pioneers besides you Pa. They had other ways of creating a frontier, and they believed that others might come after them who shared their particular vision." (Mentally, Raphael suppressed the name of Constantin Bessel before he conjured it with his tongue.) "What are we talking about here, visionaries?" Paul interjected. "History, Dad, we're talking about history." "Alright, I had no idea 'ol North Mountain harbored anyone more creative than us. That's why we're not there anymore. We're out here creating!" Raphael absorbed this in silence, and then allowed his features to assume the same grave expression he was staring at. "Back to the history. I bought the place, because it's the only way I can be sure that what I discovered even makes it into the history books, before--" "You just said the right word, son. Before. Just make sure you finish up 'before', before it's too late. You can't hold onto the place much longer. And I reckon your research had better knock a lot of socks off, because you're not likely to recover your investment in any other way!" Raphael decided to settle for a draw, lest he be asked to provide too many details. But he knew in his heart that his secret Ephraim haven was far more than a temporary holding. It was a Lighthouse in the storm.

****

On the return trip, Raphael paused long enough to visit Sophie. Privacy was at a premium for such a 'capable lass'. Nevertheless, he found consolation in her expression of regret that he was going back. "There are mysteries here too, you know. If you could just manage to be here when I'm not so busy, I'd show you some old foundations out at the Point." Much as he wanted to delay for her sake, he could not put up at the inn indefinitely, and the alternative of returning to the new homestead on the knoll was unacceptable. They settled for a token promise on his part to take her up on that sometime soon. "I'll do it anyway," she chided him gently as they parted. "Maybe I can discover a secret too!"

From there back to North Mountain seemed interminably long to him. Although he passed a greater number of outward-bound refugees on horse and on foot, he still harbored a fear that his treasure had been discovered in his absence. Though this struck him as irrational, he could not help himself. More than one property had been abandoned in the border region he was returning to; and looting was not uncommon. It was as if the famed gentility and courtesy of native Virginians only applied to holdings downstate. Anything in the wake of the current flowing out of the Old Dominion was fair game for vagabonds and squatters.

Nevertheless, he found his precautionary moorings of the house untouched, upon his arrival. But it seemed painfully clear that all of the fuss had been unnecessary. The iron grip of a frozen land pervaded everything, and Spring had reversed itself, so that even the barest attempts at new growth had been blighted. Within the only chamber he bothered to keep warm, he stoked a small kiln that more and more for him assumed the function of an alchemical oven.

The stenciled cipher on the wall now informed his efforts more from legendary hearsay than actual history; and if he could have said why, he would have admitted it was the only way to avoid concession of defeat to his father. The seed "buried in the breast" was reputed to be a grain of mystical gold, capable of converting the earth into a nascent sun.

Raphael had seen the pink boreal crown that Nature had produced for herself in the heavens of the Northwest passage. Why should not his occult predecessors have possessed a similar key? Instead of a signpost for leaving Virginia, the branch that extended out from the figure's right side spoke of how to perform a resurrection here!

Relying on his transcript of the necromantic teachings of Constantin Bessel, Raphael labored over his furnace to produce the "burning drops" of the aurum potabile. Meanwhile the earth ignored him and quietly sealed the few remaining gaps in an ice-clad reef that had grown up prodigiously around North Mountain and World's End.

As the last flurry of escapees from abandoned settlements scurried past, they barely noticed the dull forge glowing inside the frostbitten clapboard of a strange old house. And then eventually, even that smoldering spark went out, and a pervasive and crypt-like indigo descended upon the land.

****

Sophie did pay a visit to the curious foundations of the Point on a late Summer's eve. She was accompanied by the thought of a certain young man whose name was a bit hazy in her mind, although she remembered his features distinctly. He had been all about secrets, she remembered, and perhaps that was why he still retained a place among the many admirers forever seeking her company at the inn.

She highly doubted he would have found anything of interest here in her prosaic ruins. But perhaps that crude bit of carving on a post would have earned a glance from him. It seemed like a primitive attempt at a human, with some odd kind of flower design extending from the upper part of the body. She mused for but a moment longer on her memory of the effect his glances had had on her; and then, with a quick dismissal, turned her thoughts to more immediate prospects awaiting her under the rosy glow of the auroral sky.

About the Author:

Russell Yoder experienced an awakening upon first hearing the name of "Jacob Boehme" when he was a boy. While actually learning to apply the precious medicaments within Boehme's "little cabinet of divine Magia" has engaged an entire lifetime; the first and foremost ingredient has always been the necessity of holding onto a childlike heart. Over the course of a lifetime, Russell has also received teachings and empowerments within the Tibetan tradition, as well as serving for a time as the last named "Elder" within the teaching tradition of Johann Conrad Beissel, founder of the colonial Ephrata Community. Russell's previous writing on this subject was published by J.D. Holmes (2005), as "Light Dawning: Boehme, Gichtel, Ephrata, and the Origin of Rosicrucian Mysticism in the New World"; as well as his translation and introduction to American adept and friend of Ephrata, Doctor George DeBenneville's "Fasciculus: A Little Bundle, or the True and Acknowledged Universal Process of the Philosopher's Stone," published by Holmes as "An Early American Alchemical Treatise" in 2010. Translations of Henricus Khunrath's "Universal Chaos: Companion Volume to the Amphitheatre of Eternal Wisdom" and "Three Treatises of Art" (including 'Alchemy for the Behmenist Adept') followed in 2013, as Unearthed Arcana publications of Salamander & Sons; and most recently, the Institute for Hermetic Studies has issued Russell's edition of Conrad Beissel's own trance-meditations, "Wonderful Mysteries of Eternity" (2014).

Russell is now retired and living in Thailand.

A note from the Editor

Russell Robert Yoder was born in Reading Pennsylvania, 1951 to Virginia E. Russell and Robert M. Yoder. He was their second child and the eldest son with four siblings. I was his closest younger brother and as an elder brother he played a great role in my earliest thinking. I was introduced to Alchemy and the works of Jacob Boehme in the late turbulent Nineteen Sixties as well as a myriad of other fascinating topics almost too numerous to list but they included the Rosicrucians, JRR Tolkien, collecting war memorabilia at local Saturday markets, Fascism, Classical music most notably Wagner, Sibelius and Mozart, professional sports, and much much more. We were raised on a farm outside of Kutztown near a sleepy little place called Virginville on the Maiden Creek in Berks County, Pennsylvania. Both of our parents were Pa Dutch and were both born and raised in Reading. On our Father's side, ancestry ran back to some of the oldest families in the Oley Valley, the famous Swiss Yoder Brothers, Hans and Jost Joder and the Johannes Keim who recorded the first land deed in the Oley Valley. His son, Jacob's homestead has just been made a National Monument in Pike township. Our Mother's ancestry was equally old and out of Nickel Mine in Lancaster County. The name Russell was an anglicized version of Ressell originating from the Palatinate. Our Grandfather, Samuel, changed the name when registering for the draft during the First World War. Our mother to this day bless her heart, thinks she is of English descent.

Russell went to Kutztown public School and excelled in academics as well as track and field where he held the school record in the two mile event. He went to Syracuse University and received a BA in English and taught High School briefly. It was around this time that he was mentored by John Joseph Stoudt, well known author and expert on the Cloister at Ephrata. Perhaps this association lead to him going to Seminary School and becoming a UCC Minister. It was soon after this that we lost touch, I going to NYC to seek my fortune.

Forty years passed and I became friends with Mark Stavish, an incredibly knowledgeable man on the esoteric arts. Somehow Russell's name came up and through Mark, we were miraculously reconnected. Who knows how these things happen or why such is the experience of life. However the connection of blood trumps all other associations in this world and the next.

It seemed that in the interim, Russell had become the last ordained Elder at the Snow Hill Cloister, an extension of the original Ephrata Cloisters and that he was internationally acclaimed for his knowledge of Jacob Boehme, Alchemy and living in Thailand.

It was ironic that we both had been all this time mining the same Gold Mine, our Pa Dutch heritage.
And so we offer to our readers this first ever collection of my Brother, Russell R. Yoder's translations and writing.

Hunter M. Yoder, Pennsifaanische Deitsche Volkskunschtler 10/17/2018

Made in United States
Troutdale, OR
12/30/2023

16564833R00070